WILL THE
REAL
CHURCH
PLEASE
STAND UP?

WILL THE REAL CHURCH PLEASE STAND UP?

Rediscovering God's Purpose
for the Church Today

James David Montgomery

MOUNTZ
MEDIA & PUBLISHING

ISBN 978-0-9840673-9-8 // 0-9840673-9-6

Will the Real Church Please Stand Up?
Rediscovering God's Purpose for the Church Today

Published by Mountz Media & Publishing
Tulsa, Oklahoma
918.296.0995
www.mountzmedia.com

ENDORSEMENTS

As I reviewed *Will the Real Church Please Stand Up?* I realized that I was hearing from someone who has keen insights into and a great passion for what the Church can become as we mature and grow into our full, God-ordained stature. Jim Montgomery not only captures the teaching of the New Testament in his book, but also, I believe, the heart of the Lord Jesus Christ. Get ready to have your vision enlarged, and most of all, put on your marching shoes. As you read this book, I believe you'll be motivated and inspired to embark on a journey with many other believers who desire to become all that God has in mind for us.

—REV. TONY COOKE
TONY COOKE MINISTRIES
TULSA, OKLAHOMA

Great job, Jim. Though I enjoyed all of the book, my favorite chapter is "The Founding Document of the Church." This book will bring stability to a multitude of people. Thank you for your labor of love and all your hard work. This book was written for such a time as this!

—DR. MARK T. BARCLAY
PREACHER OF RIGHTEOUSNESS
MARK T. BARCLAY MINISTRIES
PASTOR, LIVING WORD CHURCH
MIDLAND, MICHIGAN

Jim's book spells out what the Church looked like and what it did in the beginning. And Jim makes the point that what the Church looked like and what it did in the first century, it ought to be doing today. Whether you stand in the pulpit or sit in the pew, you will enjoy reading about the Church that Jesus is preparing to come and take as His Bride. Jim Montgomery identifies the corrections the Church must make in order to be all that Jesus has called us to be.

—RON STAFFORD
DIRECTOR, INTERNATIONAL VICTORY BIBLE INSTITUTES,
VICTORY CHRISTIAN CENTER
TULSA, OKLAHOMA

Brother Jim Montgomery's insight into our times and Bible wisdom make *Will The Real Church Please Stand Up?* a God given gift to us all.

—LONNIE HILTON
NATIONAL DIRECTOR, FAITH CHRISTIAN
FELLOWSHIP INTERNATIONAL CHURCH
TULSA, OKLAHOMA

Jim Montgomery puts into words the concerns of many regarding the current state of our world and our church. And he takes us to the roots of our faith to show us how we can bring renewal to Christ's body. We need to hear it—and it's not complicated! Great job. Thanks Jim.

—REV. DICK SMITH
PASTOR, GOOD SHEPHERD
UNITED METHODIST CHURCH
EAST LIVERPOOL, OHIO

TO THE THREE WOMEN IN MY LIFE:

To Stephanie, my wife and my best friend,

You are truly a gift from God. I cherish you more now than the first day we met more than 45 years ago.

You are the love of my life.

To Carrie and Sarah, our daughters,

Your mother and I are so proud of you and blessed to see the devoted wives and the caring mothers you have become.

What a joy to realize you are not only our "girls," but also our best friends.

How precious you are to us!

CONTENTS

FOREWORD

Jim Montgomery and I first met more than 30 years ago when he began attending the church I pastor in Industry, Pennsylvania. Since them, Jim has entered the full time ministry and has traveled both home and abroad to proclaim the gospel and help train up pastors and leaders for the work of the Lord in today's 21st century church. Being an eye witness to his passion for truth and love for the body of Christ, it gives me great pleasure to write a few words about his first book *Will the Real Church Please Stand Up?* It's a book certain to challenge today's Church to do personal inventory to make sure it lines up with what the book of Acts reveals a New Testament church should look like.

On the day of Pentecost, the authentic ritual of the feast day was proceeding in Jerusalem with all its celebrations, traditions, decorations and readings. But, instead of falling there, the Holy Ghost chose to fall in an undistinguished upper room upon hearts that were surrendered to God and in obedience to their Savior's command. This reveals to us that God was not interested in elaborate temples of ritualism, religious professionalism, modernism or celebrated formalism. He was interested in manifesting His glory where hungry and humble hearts were willing to lay aside their religious pursuits for reality with God.

The early church was a church of purity, prayer, power and perfected praise. It was a church of believers addicted to the ministry of the saints. It was a church instructed to deny ungodliness and worldly lusts and live righteously, soberly and godly in this present world. It was a soul-winning church motivated by love.

As you open the pages of this book, block out everything that may distract you and closely listen to what the Lord wants to drop in your heart by His Spirit. Have a listening ear and allow God to open to you the windows of heaven and pour into your spirit these deep fundamental truths certain to transform your life and cause you to "stand up" and fulfill the purpose of God for the Church today.

"Unto Him be glory in the church by Christ Jesus throughout all ages, world without end. Amen" (Ephesians 3:21).

—PASTOR BILL ANZEVINO
CHRISTIAN ASSEMBLY
AN INDEPENDENT, NON-DENOMINATIONAL CHURCH
INDUSTRY, PENNSYLVANIA

PREFACE

O f all the people who have ever walked this earth, there is no question that Jesus Christ of Nazareth remains the most controversial and intriguing figure ever to have stepped on to the world stage. By every conceivable measure, His life is the most remarkable one ever lived. His ministry was revolutionary. His impact was cross-cultural, touching both Jews and Gentiles. His preaching challenged both rich and poor alike. The wisdom Jesus spoke astounded the most learned religious leaders of the day, and yet, He brought hope, help and healing to the common people.

Jesus' teachings struck a chord in the hearts of hurting, desperate people. He showed them what God is really like. You see, deep down inside every human being there exists a hunger to know the real God. There is a longing to be vitally connected with Him, to experience His presence and to enjoy a rich fellowship and relationship with the One who created us. This heart hunger that God placed within us has caused the human race to embark upon a quest to satisfy this spiritual void. Unfortunately, the inner emptiness in our souls that only God can fill has driven many people to search out and devise man-made religions.

A number of religious expressions exist in our world, each with its own unique belief system and practices, and each boasting millions of faithful adherents. Of course Islam, Buddhism,

Hinduism, Judaism and Christianity are the most widely recognized and practiced faiths, but a multitude of lesser known ones exist as well. However, even though all are very diverse and distinct faiths, still they share some similar characteristics.

One particularly predominant characteristic is that of a popular founder, one who originated the beliefs and practices constituting the fundamental tenets of the particular religion. All share a belief in a divine being who is to be obeyed and worshipped as a creator. For example, the prophet Mohammed is credited with the founding of Islam in the seventh century based on spiritual visions he claimed to have experienced. Judaism traces its origins to Moses' authorship of the Holy Scriptures, which include the Pentateuch or the first five books of the Old Testament. It is believed that Jehovah—the God of Abraham, Isaac and Jacob—inspired Moses to write these books.

Another feature already mentioned is a collection of sacred writings given to the religion's founder by God. These writings form the basis of worship and obedience by adherents to the faith. Everything needed to satisfy the religious requirements demanded by the governing deity is outlined in a sort of holy book. And it's assumed if the laws and teachings are followed, then *maybe* the faithful adherents will be accepted by the deity they attempt to please.

But friend, that is a very big *maybe*. After all, how could followers ever be totally sure that none of the religion's laws and requirements was broken? What confidence could they have that they have obeyed to the letter every statute and every commandment in the book? How could adherents be fully persuaded that they have pleased the god they were doing their best to worship and obey?

Nagging thoughts would surely resonate within a follower's mind: *Does he accept me? Does he approve of me? Have I done everything right? Have I missed the mark in any area of my life?*

These questions were at the very heart of Jesus' words recorded in Matthew 11:28 when He said, "...'Come to me, all of you who are weary and carry heavy burdens, and I will give you rest..." (NLT). The weariness and heavy burdens Jesus referred to were the laws and rules devised by the ultra-legalistic Pharisees. The Pharisees held the laws that they created and the doctrines and traditions they formed in higher esteem than the Law that God delivered to Moses.

Yet among many other things, Jesus came to remove these man-devised rules and religious decrees that bound the people so heavily and wearied them. Jesus came to declare a God of love and mercy, not a legalistic, stern, heartless taskmaster. Jesus came to reveal a God who desires relationship with His people—a God of compassion, not a God of condemnation.

I mentioned earlier that Jesus Christ is the most controversial and debatable figure in all of history. But what is it that makes Jesus so different from all other religious founders? What sets Him apart? One thing.

Jesus is the only One who ever claimed to be God.

No other spiritual leader ever made such a claim. Others may have said that they saw God, or heard the voice of God or had some kind of supernatural encounter with God. But none ever claimed to be God, or even claimed equality with God. Yet, Jesus dared to make some astounding statements that underscored His union with God. He said, "If you've seen me, you've seen the Father" (John 14:9). On another occasion He said, "I and my Father are one" (John 10:30). Jesus received honor and worship that rightly belongs only to God (Matthew 14:33; 28:9; John 5:23; Hebrews 1:6).

Jesus unashamedly claimed full equality with God. In fact, John's Gospel records a confrontation between Jesus and a group of irate Jews after Jesus healed a lame man on the Sabbath Day.

And therefore did the Jews persecute Jesus,
and sought to slay him, because he had
done these things on the sabbath day. But
Jesus answered them, My father worketh
hitherto, and I work. Therefore the Jews
sought the more to kill him, because he not
only had broken the sabbath, but said also
that God was his Father, making himself
equal with God (John 5:16-18).

If you were to ask 20 people the question, *Who is Jesus?* you likely would receive 20 different responses. Some would say He was a great religious leader. Others would call Him a prophet. Still others would regard Him as a good moral teacher who taught people about peace and love. But I like what C.S. Lewis had to say about Jesus. Oxford University professor and noted author and theologian C.S. Lewis wrote:

A man who was merely a man and said the
sort of things Jesus said would not be a
great moral teacher. He would either be a
lunatic ... or else he would be the Devil of
Hell. You must make your choice. Either this
man was, and is, the Son of God: or else a
madman or something worse.[1]

Jesus' coming was foretold long before He actually showed up. For centuries God spoke of His coming prophetically. All the major prophets in the Old Testament wrote by divine inspiration that Jesus was coming. It's been said that prophecy is history written before it happens. In other words, prophecy is God's preview of coming attractions, or news not yet taken place. In the Old Testament there are some 300 prophetic announcements heralding the coming Messiah. God spoke through the prophets that He would send to the earth a redeemer who would save the people from their sins.

One of the most startling and descriptive prophecies regarding the coming savior is recorded in the book of Isaiah:

> Therefore the Lord himself shall give you
> a sign; Behold, a virgin shall conceive, and
> bear a son, and shall call his name Immanuel
> (Isaiah 7:14).

The name Immanuel means, *God with us, God in the flesh, a man just like us.* And yet, Jesus was and is God. The New Testament describes Him this way:

> In the beginning was the Word, and the
> Word was with God, and the Word was God.
> And the Word was made flesh, and dwelled
> among us...(John 1:1,14).

His name is Jesus Christ, both a name and a title. The name *Jesus* is derived from the Greek form of the name *Jeshua* or *Joshua*, and it means, *Jehovah-Savior,* or *the Lord saves.* The title *Christ* comes from the Greek word for *Messiah* and means *anointed one*.

This God-man, Jesus, during the course of His three and a half years of ministry, prophesied that in order to fulfill the scriptures, He would suffer and be crucified and die by the hands of wicked men. But His mission was not to put Himself forth as a martyr. Rather, He willingly gave His life as a ransom for the sins of the world.

Long before being nailed to the Cross, Jesus declared that after lying dead for three days inside a borrowed tomb, He would be raised from death to resurrection life. He told His disciples He would return to heaven from whence He came and upon His arrival there, would ask the Father to send forth the Holy Spirit to indwell and empower believers. Jesus assured His followers that when the Holy Spirit came upon them, they would receive the ability to continue Jesus' ministry of preaching the gospel, teaching the good news of the kingdom of God and healing the sick.

I suppose there have been hundreds of books written about the church in the last several years, books on the subject of church history as well as those noting current trends in the church world. Articles have been written about the post-modern church, the emerging church, the Ecumenical Movement, the Charismatic Movement and many others.

Today as you scan magazine racks, bookstore shelves and airport newsstands, you can see weekly news magazine headlines touting the so-called decline of Christianity in Western society. If you believed everything written in *Time* and *Newsweek* about the current state of Christianity in America, you would think believers are abandoning their faith in Jesus Christ in record numbers. One would have the idea that the Church is in the final stages of life and dying a slow, agonizing death if all the information you had on the present state of the Church came from secular media.

But the truth is, the Church is alive and well.

It is a fact that some of the traditional, historic churches have experienced a decline of membership in the past several years, and this trend has stirred serious concern and debate among theologians and ministers. Many have speculated about the reason why once faithful parishioners are leaving their churches in record numbers.

One answer that has been given among those who've left is that church no longer seems to be something that is relevant in their lives. They have grown weary of the ritualistic formality so common in the liturgical churches that fails to address serious issues and concerns people have. Rather than being challenged to develop an intimate and ongoing fellowship with God, many believers have become weary of being subjected to a meaningless, religious form that lacks the power to truly transform their lives.

Deep down in our souls, we crave intimacy with God. We want to know that He is real and present in our lives; we want to know He truly cares about us and that He desires to connect with us in a powerful way. We long for a relationship with a God who is looking out for us and helps us in our time of need. We are desperate for a God who really knows what we're going through, a God who loves us for who we are, not just for what we can do for Him. What we don't need is the sort of sterile, detached and formal religiosity that is being served up in too many of our churches today.

There are literally thousands of Christian denominations in the world today. Each has its own unique concept of who God is, what He is really like and how He interacts with His children. Each group maintains its own view of God's nature and being. All one has to do is listen to the preaching and observe the worship practices of the various sectarian groups, and their concept of God's plan and purpose for their lives can be readily seen.

During His earthly ministry, Jesus discovered that people held many differing opinions about who He was. One day Jesus cut straight to the heart of the matter by asking a very pointed question. Jesus asked His disciples, *"Whom do men say that I the Son of Man am?"*

It's interesting that nearly everybody has an opinion about who Jesus is. The church you attend surely has a definite opinion about who He is. In fact, every Christian denomination espouses its particular view of who Jesus is. The Presbyterians, the Methodists, the Baptists, the Lutherans and the Catholics all convey by their preaching and practices the reason Jesus was sent to this earth by God. All of the great Christian churches can trace their own expression of the Christian faith to a particular person or persons such as Saint Peter, Martin Luther, John Calvin, the Wesley brothers, John Knox and others. Each of these men held to a certain interpretation and understanding of sacred scripture that in turn led to the formation of sound biblical doctrine *as they understood it*. The question that arises in the minds of many people is, "Who is the real Jesus?"

Friend, the real Jesus is the One we read about in Matthew, Mark, Luke and John. The real Jesus is the One who is the same yesterday and today and forever. For Jesus to *not* be the same today that He was 2,000 years ago when He walked the shores of Galilee, would mean He would have to change. And the Bible makes it very clear in several passages of scripture that He never changes. Malachi 3:6 says, *"For I am the Lord, and I change not."*

The ongoing legacy of Jesus' ministry is the privilege and the responsibility of the Church today. It is a ministry of proclaiming good news to the poor, announcing liberty to the captives, bringing healing to the broken hearted and reconciling fallen humanity to a just and righteous God.

Jesus made it clear that believers in each successive generation following His glorious ascension into heaven were to continue the ministry He began when He was here in the flesh. It's interesting that Luke referred to the gospel account that bears his name as being merely the *"... beginning of all that Jesus did and taught."* [7]

In the 1950s there was a popular television game show that captured the nation's attention. Three contestants stood and faced the studio audience while being asked the question: What is your name? With a straight face, all three contestants replied with the same name. The idea of the game was for the show's panelists to determine which one of the contestants was the real deal and which two were merely imposters. After asking the contestants a series of questions, each panelist selected the contestant he or she thought was the person they claimed to be.

You could feel the excitement and anticipation build as the moderator of the program ultimately asked, *Will the **real contestant** please stand up?"* One by one each contestant would begin to stand up from a seated position and then sit back down again. At last the real "John Doe" would stand up and remain standing much to the delight of the studio audience as well as the panelists.

What gave the program its popular appeal was the fact that only *one* of the contestants could rightfully claim the title; only one was the genuine article. The other two were imposters who answered questions directed to them from the panelists and were so convincing that many in the audience thought they were real. After all, they looked real. They seemed to be who they claimed to be, but only one of the three was who they purported to be.

We can apply this same parallel in the church world today. There are so many churches in America—almost one on every street corner. Yet I believe the Church in America in this 21st century has lost its way. We are like a ship ripped loose from its moorings and adrift in the sea aimlessly tossed about by every wind of doctrine.

We're being battered by waves of immorality and carnality. Prominent leaders in the body of Christ caught up in one scandal after another make the Church appear more hypocritical than ever. The world looks at us and many times sees a phony double standard. We preach one way, but we live another way. Our private lives oftentimes fail to match what we say we believe. We claim to be followers of Jesus Christ, but too often our confession of faith is nullified by the careless and indifferent way we live before the world's eyes.

Yet Jesus said that we, the Church, are the light of the world and the salt of the earth. In the same way that a lighthouse guides ships at sea safely out of dangerous fog and darkness and illuminates the way to the harbor, so we, the Church, are called to be a beacon of hope, help and healing to our generation.

It's time for the real Church to stand up and be the visible and powerful force it was intended to be. It is time for every member of Christ's body to awaken from our collective slumber, from our comfortable complacency and from our misguided ideas about what the mission of the Church is. It's time to rise up and truly *be* who we are called to be.

We have been called by Almighty God to represent Him here. The Church is nothing less than Christ's body on the earth.

> For in him dwelleth all the fullness of the Godhead bodily. And ye [the church, the collective body of Christ] are complete in him, which is the head of all principality and power..." (Colossians 2:9-10 AMP).

Will the real Church please stand up?

'I WILL BUILD MY CHURCH'

Matthew's Gospel records a critical turning point in Jesus' ministry in Chapter 16. By the time we reach this point in Matthew's narrative, Jesus had been preaching for months, and His fame had spread throughout Judea. The reports of His sermons and miracles were known far and wide, and people were divided into at least two camps.

The common people heard Jesus and gladly received His message, even if they didn't yet understand fully the principles of God's kingdom He preached. They rejoiced at the healings Jesus performed and witnessed His mighty works. People were amazed as He turned water into wine at a wedding feast in Cana, and marveled at the multiplication of the loaves and fishes from a little boy's lunch that fed at least 5,000 people on a hillside near the Sea of Galilee. The crowds who followed Jesus were in awe of Him, but they really did not know who He was. To them He was a powerful teacher and miracle worker, but nobody worshipped Him as the divine Son of God.

On the other hand, the Jewish religious leaders for the most part despised and resented Jesus. The reason for their hatred of Him was not because He was a fraud misleading the people. It was not because He preached false doctrine, for every word He spoke was truth. Their wrath toward Jesus was not based on the fact that He was a charlatan, for every healing and miracle He performed was visible and verifiable. These misguided Jewish leaders did not despise Jesus because of sin in His life, because He never committed sin of any kind.

Jesus was hated by the religious leaders because He was a threat to their selfish, vested interests. Jesus cared deeply about people, while the religious leaders cared only about their own welfare. Their chief concern was how to maintain their position of authority and control over the people. They spent much time brooding over how the common people's belief in and admiration of Jesus could threaten and diminish their place and their power.

It was apparent that a crisis was looming; something big was about to happen. And Jesus knew it. Calvary and death hung like a specter on the horizon. Soon He would be required to fulfill His role as "the lamb of God, which taketh away the sin of the world" (John 1:29). It was in the midst of this highly charged atmosphere of impending crisis, surrounded by huge crowds of supporters, and with mounting opposition against Him, that Jesus took His disciples to a place called Caesarea Philippi in northern Gentile territory.

What Jesus shared there with His followers would forever change the course of history. His death, burial and subsequent resurrection awaited Him. His time on earth was quickly coming to a close. He needed to be sure that the 12 men who followed Him so closely did, in fact, know who He was and what He expected of them *after* His departure from the world. Jesus was well aware that His disciples must take over for Him after He left and that they must be able to continue what He began.

Fully recognizing the monumental importance of training these men who would carry on His work, Jesus asked them a very direct question: "Who do men say that I the Son of man am?" They answered that some believed Him to be John the Baptist resurrected from the dead. Some believed He was Elijah or Jeremiah come back to life. Still others thought He was another of the great Old Testament prophets. But pressing the question even closer to home, Jesus wanted to know who they—His disciples—believed Him to be.

Peter, the most opinionated of the 12 and the one who habitually blurted out rash remarks, did it here again. But this time Peter was absolutely right. "...Thou art the Christ, the Son of the Living God," Peter said. His bold declaration of faith was a revelation from heaven, and Jesus told him so.

Jesus *is* the Christ, the anointed One, the Son of God in whom alone we are redeemed from the hand of the enemy. He is the Living Christ. Messiah. Redeemer. The Word made flesh. The Lamb of God. Conquering King. Jesus, Son of God and Son of man.

Responding to Peter's correct answer, Jesus said this: "I say also unto thee, That thou art Peter, and upon this rock I will build my church; and the gates of hell shall not prevail against it" (Matthew 6:18).

There has been endless debate over the precise meaning of the phrase *upon this rock*. Some have argued that the *rock* mentioned here refers to Peter. Others contend that the word *rock* is a reference to Peter's confession of faith in Jesus as the Christ. Still others believe Jesus is saying that He Himself is the rock. For the purposes of this book, I'll leave that debate to the scholars and theologians.

One thing is certain, however. Jesus is the Rock of our salvation, and the Chief Cornerstone of our faith. And those who put their trust in Him will be able to stand strong in the storms of life. Those who are a part of the Church He is building will never be defeated.

The portion of Matthew 6:18 that I wish to deal with is the last part of that verse, which says, "and upon this rock I will build my church; and the gates of hell shall not prevail against it." What a powerful statement. Think about what Jesus is saying here. The Church—whatever you and I believe it to be—is something that Jesus Himself is building. It's not being built by gifted men, a committee of theologians or even a certain denomination. Jesus Himself is building His Church.

When Jesus uttered the words *I will* in this scripture, He meant nothing will stop Him. Period. Friend, Jesus is not *thinking* about building the Church, He is *building* the Church. Jesus is not only the architect who drew up the master plan of what He is building, He is the Master Builder, the Chief Cornerstone and the sure foundation of the Church He is building.

Notice, too, that the Church Jesus is building is one in which He claims full right of ownership. It is *His* Church. And as such, He alone has the right to raise it up in the way that suits His purposes—not ours. The fact is, Jesus is the one true foundation of the Church. His blood alone purchased it, and this glorious living organism called the Church belongs to Jesus and to no other (Acts 20:28).

Again, speaking of the Church, Jesus said that the gates, or the authority, of hell itself would not be able to prevail or triumph over it. In other words, Christ will provide the means whereby His Church will never suffer defeat from any onslaught of evil hurled against it by the powers of hell. This Church will be a triumphant, victorious Church, not a weak, defenseless flock of sheep cowering in fear from the threats and intimidations of the enemy. Rather, it will be a mighty force capable of overcoming the powers of darkness. Even more importantly, the Church that Jesus is building will be the vehicle on earth God uses to expand His kingdom around the world.

What *is* this Church Jesus is building? It is the product of the death, burial and resurrection of Christ Himself. It is the offspring of a Savior who triumphed over death, hell and the grave. Jesus voluntarily left the glory of heaven to set up His kingdom in the hearts of men. He willingly paid the supreme price on the cross offering Himself as a spotless, perfect blood sacrifice to redeem mankind forever from the power and the penalty of sin.

His blood was precious blood—cleansing blood, redeeming blood. It was the only acceptable currency that heaven would ever recognize and accept as valid payment to ransom fallen humanity. When His lifeless body was taken down from the bloody cross

> **CHRIST'S TRIUMPH OVER DEATH AND HIS BEING RAISED TO NEWNESS OF LIFE UNDERSCORED THE FACT THAT SATAN'S TYRANNICAL GRIP ON THE HUMAN RACE WAS FOREVER BROKEN.**

and placed in a borrowed tomb, it lay there for three days while the debt of sin that mankind owed to a just and righteous God was being paid. Finally, when the claims of justice were fully satisfied and God accepted the offering of the blood of His holy Son as sufficient to atone for the sins of the world, Jesus was raised from the dead—*never* to die again.

The resurrection of Jesus Christ is the greatest event in all of history. Its implications are staggering, but its accomplishments have never been fully understood or appreciated in the church world. Christ's triumph over death and His being raised to newness of life underscored the fact that Satan's tyrannical grip on the human race was forever broken.

> ...He [Jesus] disarmed the spiritual rulers and authorities. He shamed them publicly by his victory over them on the cross (Colossians 2:15 NLT)

This has to do with demonic rulers and authorities.

> Forasmuch then as the children are
> partakers of flesh and blood, he also himself
> likewise took part of the same; that through
> death he might destroy him that had the
> power of death, that is, the devil (Hebrews
> 2:14).

Jesus is the only Commander-in-Chief who ever met the enemy on his own turf, on his own territory and fought the battle all by Himself. Then after waging an awful combat against all the evil principalities and powers—and even the devil himself—Jesus triumphed over all them in a decisive victory. He stripped Satan of his power over mankind. He gloriously triumphed over the prince of darkness and then awarded the spoils of victory to you and me—to His Church.

Christ's death and subsequent resurrection meant that the curse was forever broken over fallen man. The curse that entered the earth as a result of Adam's sin, a curse that involved spiritual death or separation from God, had ended. The suffering of poverty and the scourge of sickness and disease was borne by Jesus as He suffered in our place on the cross.

> Christ hath redeemed us from the curse
> of the law, being made a curse for us:
> for it is written, Cursed is every man
> that hangeth on a tree (Galatians 3:13).

We were forgiven of our sins, declared not guilty of the charges of the broken law held against us and made eternally alive in Christ.

> You were dead because of your sins and
> because your sinful nature was not yet cut
> away. Then God made you alive with Christ,
> for he forgave all our sins. He canceled the
> record of the charges against us and took it

away by nailing it to the cross (Colossians 2:13-14 NLT).

Something else happened as a result of Jesus' resurrection. He shared with His disciples that by virtue of His mighty conquest over Satan, all power and authority in heaven and in earth had been bestowed upon Him. He then conferred that same authority upon His followers.

> ...All power is given unto me in heaven and in earth. Go ye therefore, and teach all nations, baptizing them in the name of the Father, and of the Son, and of the Holy Ghost (Matthew 28:18-19).

We refer to this portion of scripture as the Great Commission. Mark also records this thought in his gospel account, but he adds another dimension we need to notice.

> And he said unto them, Go ye into all the world, and preach the gospel to every creature. He that believeth and is baptized shall be saved; but he that believeth not shall be damned. And these signs shall follow them that believe; In my name shall they cast out devils; they shall speak with new tongues; They shall take up serpents; and if they drink any deadly thing, it shall not hurt them; they shall lay hands on the sick, and they shall recover (Mark 16:15-18).

Jesus taught those who were about to take up His ministry on earth that if people will hear and accept the gospel message, they will be saved. If they don't, they will suffer eternal damnation. Jesus goes on to explain the *signs,* or the spiritual characteristics, new Christians can expect to experience in their lives. Notice that every one of these signs that will accompany believers is supernatural in nature.

Believers will be empowered to cast devils out of people being harassed and even possessed by them. They will be able to speak in new tongues, which does not refer to the natural learning of foreign languages. Rather, it means believers will be supernaturally enabled by the Holy Spirit to speak in new languages they never learned.

Jesus said another sign would be the ability to "take up serpents." This in no way has to do with the foolish practice of picking up poisonous snakes in order to prove one's great faith. If you study this verse in the original language, you will learn this phrase has the thought of exercising authority over evil spirits.

Next, Jesus deals with the promise of divine protection against intentional poisoning. Finally, the Lord promises that believers will be able to lay hands on the sick and watch them rise up well.

As you can readily see, all these signs are supernatural in origin, nature and operation. That means the ability to actuate these spiritual phenomena does not originate within the believer; these signs have a heavenly origin. They are divinely granted to the saints in order to effectively carry out the work of the Great Commission in winning people to Jesus.

Notice that Jesus said in Mark 16:17 that it was in His name that His disciples would be able to operate in spiritual manifestations. You see the phrase *in My name* quite often in the Gospels and in Acts. So it's to be regretted that in many quarters it has become something of a religious phrase as far as most of the Church is concerned. It has been largely reduced to a religious term that doesn't mean much to the average Christian.

But the fact is when Jesus uttered the words *in My Name*, He was saying, "It is by My will and by My authority that this activity be carried out in a believer's life." How important it is for us to understand that by these words Jesus is granting legal power of attorney to us to act in His name. Jesus Himself is authorizing you and me to preach, to heal and to minister in His name. The delegated authority of Christ Himself has been given us to successfully carry out the ministry of Jesus today in the place of the absent Christ.

In Mark 16 Jesus is issuing marching orders to the 12 disciples and to all those who would serve him in the future. It was their assignment, but it's ours as well. The assignment is not only to declare the glorious gospel of Jesus Christ, but also to demonstrate it. As we faithfully share the message of Jesus Christ, God promises to back up and confirm the message we speak with a tangible demonstration of His love and mercy to all who hear it and believe it. And it's all accomplished by means of the supernatural empowerment of the Holy Spirit.

Friend, this is what the Church was meant to be—a mighty wave of redeemed saints of God preaching the gospel of Christ, clothed with Holy Spirit power, marching forth throughout the earth liberating suffering, dying humanity from the bondage of the enemy. The Church was never intended to be a weak, wimpy, denominationally brainwashed bunch of defenseless lambs who can't fight their way out of a wet paper bag, spiritually speaking.

The Church that Jesus is building is one that all of hell cannot defeat. It's a Church that was birthed not by a man, but by *the* man—The Man Christ Jesus (1 Timothy 2:5).

However, herein lies the problem. We have settled for such a low level of Christianity for so long, it has become the norm. Something terrible has happened to the belief system we call Christianity over the past centuries since that first century church shook the prevailing religious world to its very foundations. We allowed it to become a religion. We took a message that made it possible for people to receive eternal life—God's very own life— and allowed it to degenerate into a system of man-made rules and regulations. A careful study of church history shows that each successive generation of believers since those first century believers have introduced their own brand of doctrines and traditions that many times are at odds with the scriptures.

Let's be honest here. We all have our own opinions about the Word of God. We all have views about the interpretation of certain scripture passages. We've learned to accept these views from a variety of sources: our church affiliation, from pastors who've preached to us and taught us Bible truths and from the particular perspective to which our favorite Bible teachers subscribe. Add in seminary or Bible school training we may have received, and it's easy to see why there's such a diversity of opinion as to what the Church is, what should constitute its activities and by what means those activities should be carried out and accomplished.

That's the thing about opinions; everybody has one. A well-known minister was discussing a Bible subject one day in a church service. A member of this particular church approached the minister after the service and voiced his disagreement with the minister's teaching, even though the minister had underscored his sermon with several scriptural proofs.

"Well, everyone has a right to his or her opinion about the Bible," the church member objected.

"No, dear brother, everyone has a right to believe and obey the Bible," the minister responded.

You see, we are not called to preach our opinion about the Word of God. Neither are we instructed to preach personal convictions concerning cultural and social matters such as clothing styles, what we should eat and what we should avoid eating, etc. Instead, the apostle Paul exhorted Timothy, his son in the faith, to "preach the Word." Timothy was not instructed to preach his opinions, pet doctrines or the latest wind of doctrine blowing through the church world. He was admonished by Paul to preach the Word.

The Church in Acts preached the Word and witnessed remarkable results as the incorruptible seed of that Word was planted in the hearts of men and women. Sinners received eternal life, the sick and afflicted were healed, the demon-possessed were set free, those bound by occult practices and witchcraft were so gloriously delivered by the power of God that they voluntarily burned the books that taught them Satanic black arts.

All of this happened as a result of the fearless preaching of God's Word. Jesus had cautioned earlier in one of His sermons about the negative consequences associated with substituting God's clearly revealed Word with ideas and doctrines of men.

> But in vain do they worship
> me, teaching for doctrines the
> commandments of men (Matthew 15:9).

If something is done in vain, that means it was accomplished, but it did not produce anything worthwhile or lasting. The results were very different than what we hoped they would be. Jesus charged the Pharisees and the scribes, the religious leaders who opposed Him the most, with not only rejecting the commandments of God, but also of exalting their own man-made traditions and rules *above* the Word of God. That was indeed a very serious indictment against their religious pride and prejudice. They were guilty of willfully discarding God's commandments, and instead embracing and putting forth their own.

It's amazing how you can read the Bible for years and still miss some important information God intended us to receive. We've all done it. A portion of scripture that we have read countless times will one day seem to leap off the page and register on our hearts in a way we never before experienced. That is nothing less than the Holy Spirit bringing fresh revelation of truth to enlighten and encourage us.

In my experience one of those verses was found in Luke 24:49. Here, Jesus commanded His disciples, the ones who would inherit the ministry Jesus began, to tarry or to wait in Jerusalem before they began their program of evangelizing the world. Jesus told them to proclaim the gospel to every creature, but not to do it yet!

Why would He tell them to wait? Surely Jesus knew the desperate peril sinners faced in their lives apart from receiving His gospel. There was no doubt Jesus understood the urgency of the hour. Why would He of all people be the one to tell them to wait? Because Jesus understood the importance of being fully equipped and empowered to share His good news with hurting humanity. The disciples simply were not ready yet; they needed more equipment before they could begin. They had received a commission, but they had not yet received the power.

Jesus knew if they were to pick up where He left off, they must have the same ability He had when He taught in their synagogues and preached the gospel of the kingdom. They would need to have the same power that enabled Jesus to open blind eyes, cleanse lepers, heal the lame and exercise authority over demons. That's why Jesus instructed them to wait for an enduement, or a clothing of power, from heaven. Jesus told them to wait for the coming of the Holy Spirit, an event He often spoke of in His private time with the disciples.

Among other things, Jesus promised His disciples that the Holy Spirit would be to them, and to us, another Comforter. In other words, everything Jesus was to them when He was with them in person, the Comforter, the Holy Spirit, would be to them in His absence. The Holy Spirit would accompany them, lead them, empower them for service, warn them of impending danger and embolden them. Knowing that the Holy Spirit would be an indispensable Helper in their ministry, Jesus urged His disciples to wait and receive this measure of the Spirit of God coming upon them.

Again in Acts 1:8 Jesus reiterates the importance of waiting for the coming Holy Spirit. Here Jesus commands the disciples to "wait for the promise of the Father." A commandment of the Lord is something that is not open for discussion. A commandment of God means that the Lord has His mind made up on the subject. He knows what we need. He knows what is best. And He knows what works.

We do not have the right to take a commandment of the Lord and treat it as an *option*. Options are fine if we're talking about buying a new car and considering extra equipment and conveniences we'd like to enjoy on our new vehicle; it's ours, and we can choose whatever we want. But friend, when it comes to the ministry of Jesus Christ— and the liberation of hurting people who need to hear about and receive a Redeemer who loves them and gave His life for them—we need to humble ourselves and be willing to do things in ministry His way.

THE CHURCH IS PRESENTLY IN FULL POSSESSION OF ALL THE RESOURCES AND SUPPLY THAT JESUS HAD WHEN HE WAS HERE.

As disciples of the Lord Jesus, we have become His empowered agents on the earth. We read of occasions when Jesus sent His disciples out on preaching missions. In doing this He was, in effect, extending His own work in the Galilee region.

> And when he had called unto him his twelve disciples, he gave them power against unclean spirits, to cast them out, and to heal all manner of sickness and all manner of disease (Matthew 10:1).

Today Jesus is physically absent from the world, but the Church is now Christ's body on the earth. Believers have been granted the power of attorney to act on His behalf in order that the same work Christ started may be continued with the same results He had. The Church is presently in full possession of all the resources and supply that Jesus had when He was here. *Everything* Jesus had available to Him in His earthly ministry of teaching, preaching and healing is now at the disposal of the Church.

It's interesting to note that Jesus' disciples were well aware of the *facts* of the gospel, as well as the facts of Christ's resurrection for some 50 days after Jesus had been raised from death. But it took something more than merely a dry recitation of these facts to persuade people of the life-changing claims of the gospel. It would require anointed preaching backed up by supernatural confirmation of the Word if people were to be convinced that Jesus was indeed alive.

Jesus fully understood this fact, and He knew it would take nothing less than the baptism of the Holy Ghost to empower His disciples to accurately and effectively represent the risen Lord Jesus. These men and women would not be just preachers. They must also be His *ambassadors*. An ambassador is one who is qualified to represent a nation or kingdom in a foreign land. The ambassador does not present his own views and interests. Rather, he is an advocate for the views and policies of the nation that sent him. He does not represent himself. He doesn't act on his own accord. He has authority and credentials given him by the sending nation to act on *its* behalf.

The Church that Jesus is building is not composed of independent envoys, each doing their own thing and putting forth their own ideas. We are Christ's ambassadors. As such, we represent, we stand in the place of the One who has sent us forth. We bear the King's message, not our own. We have been entrusted with the most revolutionary message the world has ever heard at any time in history.

We're not called to explain it. We're not expected to prove it or defend it. God is well able to watch over His Word to perform it. He is the One who will bring it to pass. Our responsibility as believers is simply to deliver the message—the gospel. What is the gospel?

> For I am not ashamed of the gospel of Christ:
> for it is the power of God unto salvation to

every one that believeth; to the Jew first,
and also to the Greek (Romans 1:16).

Paul was inspired by the Holy Spirit to write that the gospel is the power of God. Dr. C.I. Schofield, a notable conservative Baptist theologian and author of the widely used Schofield Bible, made this interesting observation about the word "salvation" in the above verse in Romans. He said:

> The Greek and Hebrew words for salvation imply the ideas of preservation, soundness, wholeness, safety and healing. Salvation is the great inclusive word of the Gospel, gathering unto itself all the redemptive acts and processes.[1]

The mission of the Church is to declare Christ's salvation. Our job is to present the gospel in all its fullness to people. We are witnesses of Jesus Christ—ordinary men and women—who do extraordinary things by the supernatural equipping of the Holy Spirit. Remember, Jesus is the One who said that He would pray the Father to send forth the Holy Spirit to indwell believers. But Jesus clearly taught that once the Holy Spirit came on the Day of Pentecost, He would not only dwell within believers, He would also rest upon them in power.

If Jesus did not want His Church to receive this clothing of power from on high, then why did He promise it? As the head of the Church it was His prerogative to withhold supernatural ability from His Church if He'd wanted it that way. But He didn't want it that way; He withheld nothing. He is the One building the Church, and He has the right to build it any way He sees fit. He can equip and arrange its members any way He wants. But clearly He has chosen to build it and furnish it in a manner that will produce the greatest results. He has chosen to anoint His disciples with the very same anointing with which He Himself was anointed.

> How God anointed Jesus of Nazareth with the Holy Ghost, and with power, who went about doing good, and healing all that were oppressed of the devil; for God was with him (Acts 10:38).

That was the key to Jesus' miracles of healing and all the mighty acts He performed. He was anointed with the Holy Ghost and with power. And He told those who would continue His work that they would also receive the same power from the same Holy Spirit that He had. Just imagine—the same power Jesus Himself possessed, but now that power would emanate from ordinary men and women. Friends, this is New Testament. This is the heritage and the legacy of the Church.

Yet for years this idea of the baptism of the Holy Spirit has caused a firestorm of controversy in the church world. The supernatural gifts or endowments that have been given to the Church, the supernatural ability to speak in tongues as the Spirit gives utterance, divine healing and the ability to cast out devils has ignited more theological battles than can be counted.

You can talk about God and people won't mind. You can talk about Jesus and believers will smile. But if you mention the Holy Ghost, people get nervous. Bring up the subject of speaking in tongues and Christians will look at you like you just hopped off a spaceship from another planet. Or, they'll get defensive and upset about it. But why in the world should we be upset about something Jesus promised us?

Someone might say, "Well, I just believe those things died out with the last apostle in the early church." Others say, "I believe that miracles and all those supernatural occurrences were necessary to get the church started. But once the canon of scripture was completed, we don't need to expect those kinds of things to operate in the church anymore. We have Bibles now."

Maybe you've heard those kinds of opinions; I know I have. I've heard them from fellow Christians as well as theologians, well-known Christian ministers and best-selling authors. But there's a big problem. Comments like those cannot be supported by scripture, and the Word of God must be the bottom line for our faith and practice as believers. (We'll deal with this all-important subject in a later chapter.)

I said earlier that we allowed Christianity to become *TRUE* relegated to a religion. By that I mean it has evolved from the time of the first century church into a complicated and often man-made set of dogmas and beliefs that sometimes are at odds with the rightly divided Word of God. It's interesting that the word *religion* comes from the Latin root word *religare*, which means, "to bind anew, to bind back, to bind again." Too many *TRUE* times that's exactly what religion does in people's lives. It binds them, restrains them and holds people in the grip of humanly devised beliefs that have little or nothing to do with God's Holy Word or His plan for people's lives.

The book of James talks about a religion that is pure and undefiled before God (James 1:27). So you can readily see that there's a religion according to the scriptures that honors God, obeys God and is acceptable to God. The problem arises when we begin to inject a mix of our own theories about God's Word along with some of our own natural human reasoning. That's when religion turns into something that binds us and limits us as the Latin root word suggests.

When the Church attempts to function without the help of the mighty Holy Spirit, it becomes bound. A believer who tries to live the Christian life without the baptism in the Holy Ghost is a believer whose life will be impeded and confined. I know. I tried it and it didn't work. And so have many, many others.

I was a Christian, a believer. I was born again. If I had died, I would have gone to heaven—no doubt about it. But I was defeated and sick most of the time. My wife, Stephanie, and I loved the Lord, and we both made confessions of faith in Christ. We were trying to live the Christian life, but the truth is we weren't having much victory in our lives at all. We struggled. We served God the best we knew how, and we went to church. When we did, we'd feel close to God during the service, but we had no lasting joy or peace in our lives. We were so perplexed.

Something was missing. Something wasn't right. We wanted more out of our relationship with God, but we didn't have a clue how to get it. After all, if you don't know what's missing, how would you know when you got it? I can remember nights in bed reading a paraphrase of the New Testament that was very popular in the late 1960s and early 1970s titled Good News for Modern Man.

I would read Paul's epistles to the Church, but I didn't have a clue what he was talking about. Here I was reading these letters to the churches in a translation of the Bible written in modern language, but still I had no idea what Paul was attempting to communicate to the young churches he pioneered. I was totally in the dark. I read the words on the pages, but I failed to understand the thought God was trying to deliver to these first believers and to me.

I was frustrated and confused. I simply could not wrap my mind around the truths on the pages of the New Testament. All this took place during a time when Stephanie and I were hungry for more of God. We were on a quest to know Him more. We wanted more of God, but we had no idea how to receive more of what He had to offer us.

Looking back on those days some 30 years ago, I can promise you something: If you hunger and thirst for more of God, the

Lord will see to it that you won't walk away empty-handed. Jesus said those who hunger and thirst after righteousness will be filled (Matthew 5:6). If you're hungry for more of God, He will fill you! If you're thirsty for more of His refreshing presence, He will give it to you. He did with Stephanie and me, and He will do it for you too.

What we didn't realize was that the very thing we needed to satisfy the longing and the emptiness in our Christian experience already had been provided for us. It is what Jesus referred to as the promise of the Father. It's the promise of God that belongs to every born-again child of God: the blessed Holy Spirit in all His fullness within and resting upon every child of God.

> And, behold, I send the promise of my
> Father upon you: but tarry ye in the city of
> Jerusalem, until ye be endued with power
> from on high (Luke 24:49).

The Lord sent two wonderful Spirit-filled Catholic Christians into our lives one day to share the truth from God's Word about the baptism of the Holy Spirit with us. They read from the scriptures to us about this experience. As they did, our hearts bore witness with the truth they shared with us, and we eagerly received the message they brought into our home that day just like the believers in Ephesus in Acts 19 and just like Saul of Tarsus (later Paul the apostle) in Acts 9.

When hands were laid upon us and prayer was made for us, Stephanie and I received the same Holy Spirit those in Acts had received, in the same way they received and with the same evidence they experienced. We immediately began to speak in other tongues just like they did. We received a beautiful and heavenly prayer language given us by the Holy Spirit that enabled us to express to God in spiritual language what our English language was not sufficient to fully express to Him.

41

From that day on our lives began to change dramatically. We sensed a new joy, a new boldness, and a new love for God's Word began to take hold in our lives. Our thinking was gradually being changed. We no longer felt like victims. We sensed a new strength emerging within us. The Bible became a new book to us. We began to understand what God had been trying to say to us all along. We learned that in the same way Jesus was God's gift to the world, so the Holy Spirit is God's gift to His Church.

WITHOUT THE ADDED DIMENSION OF THE BAPTISM OF THE HOLY SPIRIT IN OUR LIVES, INSTEAD OF BELIEVERS PREVAILING OVER THE POWERS OF DARKNESS, THE ENEMY WILL RUN ROUGHSHOD OVER BELIEVERS.

Without the added dimension of the baptism of the Holy Spirit in our lives, instead of believers prevailing over the powers of darkness, the enemy will run roughshod over believers. Why? Because it takes more than human ability, willpower, might and wisdom to be able to successfully carry out Christ's command to go into all the world and make disciples of all nations. It requires an unceasing flow of the Holy Spirit in our lives to exercise dominion over the works of the enemy.

> So he answered and said to me: "This is the word of the Lord to Zerubbabel: 'Not by might nor by power, but by My Spirit,' Says the Lord of hosts (Zechariah 4:6 NKJV).

An angel appeared to Zechariah and showed him a vision of a lampstand with a large bowl on top of it. Two olive trees stood on either side of the bowl, from which flowed an unceasing supply of oil into the bowl. The oil, in turn, provided a continuous aura of light in the temple. The angel asked Zechariah if he understood the meaning of the vision. "No, my lord," Zechariah replied.

Consider again carefully the angel's response to Zechariah, "...Not by [human] might, nor by [human] power, but by my spirit, Says the Lord of hosts.

In other words it will take the oil, a symbol or type throughout scripture of the anointing or empowerment of the Holy Spirit, to provide the energy that effectively accomplishes God's work on earth. It won't be human might or ability, but God flowing through a consecrated human vessel. It will be God and man laboring together to reap a harvest of souls for whom Jesus suffered, bled and died to ransom. It's not God alone, and it's certainly not man alone that gets the job done, but it is God working through His redeemed sons and daughters, demonstrating His love and compassion toward hurting humanity.

It's interesting that later in this same chapter, Zechariah asked the angel a question: "What are these two olive trees on either side of the lampstand?" Notice again the angel's response.

> Then said he, These are the two anointed ones, that stand by the Lord of the whole earth (Zechariah 4:14).

The olive trees yielded the oil that flowed without ceasing into the lampstand, which in turn, provided a steady stream of light into the temple. But notice that the angel explained that the trees actually represented two men: Joshua, the high priest, and Zerubbabel, the Prince of Judah. Here again we see the duality of God and His anointed man—His vessel—laboring together to bring a manifestation of His saving, healing and delivering power to the sons of men. We see God's holy oil—typifying the anointing of the Holy Spirit, the quickening power of the Living God—flowing through a human vessel.

The fact is, God has always looked for a man—one He could partner with in the earth. God has looked for a man who would obey Him, walk with Him and be that vessel through whom He could freely pour Himself through as rivers of Living Water to help, heal and bless people bound in darkness.

I sought for a man (Ezekiel 22:30).

Elijah was a man (James 5:17).

It's important to understand that in the Old Covenant provision was made by God for a select class of people to experience God's anointing of the Holy Spirit: the priest, the prophet and the king. But even they did not posses this anointing as an ongoing, continual enduement of power in their lives.

> But, thank God, today we can. The Church—
> you and I—by virtue of the baptism in the
> Holy Spirit can experience a power that is
> not of this world but of heaven. This infilling
> of divine power is not just a one-time
> experience that we look back on as an event
> in our lives with no bearing upon today.
> Rather, it's meant to be an ever-present
> flow of living water that refreshes us with
> His presence and equips us with His power.
>
> In the old dispensation men experienced
> divine power; in the new they received
> power. In the old they responded to power;
> in the new He gives them power (Luke
> 10:19). The Holy Ghost descended upon
> men before Pentecost; today, since that
> heaven descending cloudburst, He saturates
> and fills them (Acts 2:4,8). [2]

The Church that Jesus is building is made up of His empowered agents, His representatives. Think with me for a moment of the scripture in 1 Corinthians 3.

> For we are laborers together with God: ye
> are God's husbandry, ye are God's building
> (1 Corinthians 3:9).

Notice this scripture does not say that God is laboring together with us. It says we are laboring together with Him. That means He is the One who calls the shots; He is the One in charge. He's making the decisions and determining the work that is to be done and how it's to be carried out.

That work is nothing less than the rescue and the recovery of perishing humanity. Actually, that's what the Church is—a search and rescue team. We're to search the highways and byways of life looking for those who've lost their way. We're to seek out the lonely, the addicted, the bound and hurting masses of people and let them know there's One who knows their hurt and pain. There is One who is aware of the sin and evil that binds them with chains. There is One who voluntarily took their place and bore their sins. There is One who died as their substitute in order to set them free.

When Jesus ministered on earth, the Bible says that He was moved with compassion toward the needs of the people. He viewed people as vulnerable sheep without a shepherd—hungry, hurting, confused and in need of someone to lift them up.

When Jesus met folks whose lives were scarred by sin, He didn't condemn them. He ministered to them. Yet, He did it in a way that filled them with hope, letting them know that God was not willing that they perish in their sins. Jesus' message to sinners was that there was a way out for them. They no longer had to remain shackled by fetters of sin, sickness disease and poverty. He didn't condone their sin, but He didn't condemn them either. He showed them a better way.

...Ye are God's building (1 Corinthians 3:9).

The Church Jesus is building shares His same concern for the lost. His Church has the same compassion for the sick and suffering that He did, and it has the same supernatural power to effectively minister as Jesus had. This Church is one that is not ashamed of the gospel of Christ and not ashamed of the One in whom this glorious gospel is all about. This Church is not ashamed to share its life-changing power with those who need it the most, and it's not afraid to demonstrate the supernatural signs and wonders God uses to confirm the message we preach.

We are the Church Jesus was talking about in Matthew 16:18. We are the Church that hell cannot prevail against. We are a people called out from the world, called out of darkness, called out of defeat and failure. And we are the Church that Jesus is building, equipping, empowering and overseeing.

CHAPTER 2

THE FOUNDING DOCUMENT OF THE CHURCH

There is no place on earth I would rather call home than this great nation of ours. I love the United States of America. Even with all its flaws and imperfections, the United States continues to shine forth as an enduring beacon of freedom and liberty to oppressed people around the world.

When European immigrants began streaming into America in the early 20th century, the Statue of Liberty was the first symbol of the New World these newcomers gazed upon as the ships bearing new citizens-to-be steamed into New York Harbor. Following the long, arduous trans-Atlantic voyage inside crowded ship quarters and from the decks of those great ocean-going vessels, these new settlers looked with awe and wonder at the imposing and magnificently beautiful Lady Liberty.

When they looked at her they saw much more than a large statue made of metal. They saw a symbol of freedom, equality, justice and opportunity. It didn't matter what country they came from or how low their place was on the social ladder. When they gazed at her holding high the torch of freedom, it was as if they heard her welcome them with these words: "Here you can begin a new life. There is opportunity here. You can be free. You can succeed. You can climb as high as your dreams will take you. If you are willing to work hard, you can be anything you want to be. This is America, the land of the free and the home of the brave."

I believe America is great for many reasons. We became great when people came here from Europe in the 1600s fleeing religious tyranny that mandated state-controlled worship. Early pilgrims were willing to endure the rigors of rough sea travel to forge a new life in a land where they could be free to worship God according to the Holy Scriptures and not in accordance with the unjust laws of the land or the whims of a royal monarchy.

America is great because of our system of government. It's a government *of* the people, *by* the people and *for* the people. It's a representative democracy and a government in which we freely choose our leaders not to rule over us with an iron fist, but to represent us in the halls of Congress, state houses and city halls.

America is a fundamentally good, decent and benevolent nation. Time and time again we have come to the aid of nations around the world in their times of need and in times when they were being threatened by foreign aggressors. We have heard the cries of people suffering under the burden of oppressive dictatorships and have answered them by coming to their aid and lending our support. We sent young Americans to fight side by side with them in order to throw off the bonds of tyranny and help them gain their freedom.

America is great because we have sent more men and women abroad on the mission fields of the world to proclaim the good news to people than any other nations. We are by no means the only country that has dispatched missionaries to the far-flung corners of the earth. Many nations have sent Christian workers abroad to tell the story of Jesus Christ, but not in the numbers that America has.

Finally, I believe the United States is great because of our founding documents—the proclamations and writings that serve as our nation's official birth certificates. These are the documents that define us as a nation. They tell us who we are and what America is all about. Collectively, they form the vision statement of the United States of America. They spell out our purpose for being, our goals, our rights as citizens and how those rights are to be protected by law.

The Declaration of Independence, the Constitution and the Bill of Rights are the writings that serve as the supreme law of the land. These are the very foundation and source of the legal authority underlying the existence of the United States and our federal government. They are the writings that provide the framework for the organization and the administration of our government.

We've all studied these historic documents in school. We all know something about them, or at least we did at one time. Yet, it would be good if we as American citizens would take the time to re-read these documents and remind ourselves of the genius of our founding fathers in creating a nation based on law and high principle. It would be worthwhile to realize the reliance upon God's guidance and the recognition of His divine providence that moved these great men in the crafting of these documents. The men who signed their names to the Declaration of Independence, thus signifying their agreement to the principles contained in it, pledged their *"lives, their fortunes and their sacred honor."* BE WISE TO REMEMBER THIS

And yet, in much the same way that these documents serve as the blueprint for the establishment of the United States, there is a corresponding document that serves as the founding document of the Church. It is none other than the New Testament book of Acts, which is the blueprint for the founding of the Church given to us by the hand of God. And it is the vision statement of a Church in action. Acts outlines the creation, the activities, the makeup, the power behind and the mandate given to the Church of Jesus Christ.

It clearly sets forth how the Church came into being, when it came into being, what the Church is, who comprises its members, and more importantly, why the Church exists in the first place. You see, without this divine record of the supernatural birth and subsequent activities of this young Church in Acts how could we possibly fully understand God's purpose for the body of believers united in Jesus Christ that we call *the Church?*

There are hundreds of thousands of churches in the United States today with millions of Christians in their ranks. I'm convinced the majority of church members are those who have become "born again." They have experienced the impartation of God's life and nature into their hearts or spirits, thus transforming them into what the Bible calls new creations.

Yet, even though churches are filled with people who have received the new birth and are performing good works and are truly committed to the Lord, still we cannot know with absolute certainty that these assemblies of believers are carrying on the work God had in mind when He birthed the Church on the Day of Pentecost.

Your church or mine may or may not be what God planned when He sent forth the sound of a rushing, mighty wind from heaven accompanied by cloven tongues of fire that rested upon each of the 120 disciples gathered in that upper room. To the degree that our churches today correspond and reflect the energy, zeal and supernatural equipping of the Holy Spirit—and carry out the ministry template of the Acts church—to that degree alone will our churches fulfill God's design for the Church.

It is not my intention to arouse controversy or to criticize any house of worship in America. I am not attempting to create any further schisms within the body of Christ. And it is not my purpose to tear down the Church. My goal is to awaken Christians everywhere to the glorious heritage left us in the scriptures. I firmly believe that once we see where we came from and observe the world-changing impact the first century church had in its day, we will be determined to rise up in faith and *be* that Church in our day.

There are many voices in the Christian world today saying that we must redefine the Church to make it more compatible with popular culture. Many believe church must become more relevant in a society that has become increasingly secular. These observers recognize that society is less traditional in its thinking and more open minded when it comes to things like morality, to what constitutes right and wrong, and therefore, they believe the church should reflect this evolution.

> **THE CHURCH DOES NOT NEED TO BE REDEFINED. IT NEEDS TO BE REDISCOVERED, AND ITS PURPOSE AND CALLING RESTORED IN THIS 21ST CENTURY.** *AGREE*

But the fact is, the Church does not need to be redefined. It needs to be *rediscovered*, and its purpose and calling restored in this 21st century.

Frankly, the Church has lost its way. And we have allowed it. We have allowed this great living offspring of the death, burial and resurrection of Jesus Christ to degenerate into an irrelevant, worn-out religious machine. We're using the wrong scoreboard to determine how we're faring in the struggle raging between the forces of God and good and His arch-enemy, Lucifer, and the evil he brings to bear upon the human race.

Too many times we are concerned with externals that have little or nothing to do with the mission of the Church. We're hung up on the size of our church buildings and how beautifully they're furnished. We provide state-of-the-art, computer-generated digital graphics on mega-sized screens to display the words to our worship songs. Pastors brag to one another about the size of their congregations. We pride ourselves on our programs and events. We're keeping everybody busy. If we have lots of money in the treasury, we think that's a sign of success.

It's certainly not wrong to have a large building. Lyrics on a big screen are fine. Thank God for lots of people in the building; it sure beats not having enough. But it's interesting to me that the church in Acts didn't have a carpeted platform, an expensive pulpit or a public announcement system. The church didn't have polished, professional preachers, fancy programs, a fine building, a big budget or a hefty bank account.

But it had power! It had the delegated power and authority of Christ Jesus Himself. When the Holy Spirit was poured out upon the 120 people gathered together on the Day of Pentecost, God filled the room and then He filled the people. Those waiting disciples became God's living temples. God moved out of a temple made by man's hands and He took up residence in temples made by His hands. On that glorious day that marked the birth of the Church, the Holy Spirit not only came to indwell believers, but He came also to anoint them with supernatural enablement to do the same works Jesus had done. The result? They went forth preaching, teaching, healing and ministering to people. God showed Himself through men.

We see this concept of God working and ministering through people in the first few verses of the book of Acts.

> The former treatise [or in his first writing,
> which was Luke's gospel account] have I
> made, O Theophilus, of all that Jesus began
> both to do and to teach (Acts 1:1).

Here, Luke sets the tone and lays the groundwork for the entire book of Acts by explaining something very important. He shows the Bible reader that the Gospel of Luke describes what Jesus *began* to do during His earthly ministry, while in Acts we see what Jesus *continued* to do on earth through His body after

He returned to heaven. The difference is that throughout the book of Acts we do not read of Jesus in His physical body continuing to walk the earth. Jesus was no longer on earth at that point. So how did He continue His ministry? Jesus continued teaching, preaching, healing and exercising authority over demons *through the Church*. Jesus accomplished His ministry through Peter, Paul, Silas, Stephen, Phillip, John Mark, Barnabas and a host of others—some who were apostles and some who were not.

There is a phrase Paul uses in one of his epistles that best describes the Church:

> ...the Church, Which is his body, the fulness of
> him that filleth all in all (Ephesians 1:22-23).

What does the phrase, "the Church which is His body" mean? It means that Christ's ministry is now being enacted through His body, the Church. It's not a different ministry than the one Jesus performed when He was on the earth; it's the same ministry. The difference is that now the Church is empowered by Christ Himself to do not only the same works Jesus did, but also to do even greater works (John 14:12).

People all over the world are desperate to hear about a Jesus who still saves the lost, opens blind eyes, unstops deaf ears and makes the lame walk and leap for joy. And when they hear the good news presented with the same passion, the same boldness, the same conviction and the same faith with which the early church shared these mighty truths, Jesus will step out of the pages of the Bible and do the same thing in their lives that He did 2,000 years ago.

Someone might say, "But my denomination doesn't believe in speaking in tongues. We don't believe in miracles or divine healing. My pastor and my group don't believe those things are for us today." This kind of thinking reminds me of a certain famous fast food franchise that ran a successful advertising campaign a number of years ago. The slogan in its commercials was *"Have it your way."*

The company wanted you to know that you could have your hamburger prepared and garnished any way you wanted. But the truth is, while that may work when it comes to hamburgers, it doesn't work when it comes to God's Church. If you are going to walk in the fullness of God's Word, you don't get to pick and choose portions of the Bible you want to believe and enact in your life.

The blueprint for the Church has already been drawn. The founding document of the Church already has been drafted. None of us has the right to go through pages of scripture like we go through the line of our favorite buffet restaurant choosing items we like and ignoring those we don't like.

The book of Acts is the official record of the Church fulfilling the purpose for which it was created in the first place. The Church is a mighty wave of redeemed saints of God marching forth in the power of the Holy Spirit proclaiming a *supernatural* message about a *supernatural* Redeemer with *supernatural* ability.

Acts is the inspired Word of God chronicling the actions of fearless men and women committed to bear the message that Jesus preached. They proclaimed the One who with His own blood demolished the wall of separation between God and man—a wall that sin and disobedience erected. It was a chasm so wide and so deep between the Creator and His creation that nothing less than the blood of Jesus was sufficient to repair the breach that sin had created.

Where are the rugged men and women of faith in our day who are willing to lay down their lives to let the whole world know that Jesus saves, Jesus heals, Jesus delivers and Jesus is coming again? Where are the people in our day who will pick up where those emboldened witnesses of the early church left off? People who "loved not their lives unto the death," or as some Bible translations write, "they were willing to die...," "... they

54

did not cling to life…," "…they did not hold their lives too dear to lay them down…" and "…they loved not their lives even in the face of death." WERE REBELS FoR JESUS

These pioneer disciples realized—as I fear many in the Church today do not—that when Jesus bought us with His precious life we died to the things of this world. At the moment of our new birth, we were crucified to the things this world has to offer: the lust of the flesh, the lust of the eyes and the pride of life. We're no longer to be governed by these things like unsaved people. Instead, we're to be governed by a new law—the law of the spirit of life in Christ Jesus. We're to be governed by the love of God and the faith of God.

Keep in mind that the book of Acts portrays people who walked according to this new law, and yet, they were ordinary people just like you and me accomplishing extraordinary things. They were common people accomplishing uncommon things. These believers were the people of God called by His name. They were indeed a new breed of people, the likes of which the world had never seen before. They completely baffled the religious leaders of the day.

Here were people who were truly the salt of the earth. They were fishermen, laborers and a despised tax collector, but they were extraordinary in God just the same. Nothing in their backgrounds qualified them for the mighty works they performed in Jesus' name. Nothing in their upbringing prepared them for the mighty Word of God they preached. It wasn't their seminary training or their social pedigree that commanded the attention of the people who heard and saw them.

So what, then, were their credentials? Quite simply, they had been with Jesus. And that was enough—it was more than enough. They walked with Jesus. They ate with Him and slept near Him. They walked the hot, dusty roads of the Middle East with Him. They formed His crusade team. They heard every one of His sermons, and then enjoyed the benefit of His personally expounding and enlarging upon the words He preached to the multitudes. They saw the miracles He did. They asked Him questions, and He answered them. And all the while He was training them, He was also preparing to entrust them with His ministry that had to continue after His departure.

Perhaps they were not familiar with every nuance of the Law like the Pharisees were, but they had learned well in the school of Christ, and Jesus had personally given them power to do the same works He had done. Jesus was no longer present with them in the physical sense, yet He was very much with them through the person of the Holy Ghost. So while these apostles may not have understood every jot and tittle—every Hebrew letter of the Torah or the writings of the prophets like the scribes and Pharisees did— still, they had spent time with the One called *"the Word of God."*

The Book of Acts does not record the deeds of perfect people. Christians were not perfect then nor are they now. We read of squabbles between the apostle Paul and his traveling companion, Barnabas, regarding the issue of young John Mark accompanying them on a missionary journey (Acts 15). Peter was called on the carpet in Jerusalem by the elders of the young church. These leaders, all of them Jewish believers, were horrified that Peter would dare preach Jesus Christ to the Gentiles (Acts 11).

There are doctrinal conflicts recorded (Acts 15). There are accounts of unscrupulous individuals who tried to lie to God about the amount of money given in an offering (Acts 5). We are informed of a man who attempted to purchase with money the anointing of the Holy Spirit (Acts 8). All of these situations underscore the fact that this mighty Church in the first century was by no means a perfect one. There were flawed individuals in this Church. Yet that fact did not prevent the vast majority of believers from carrying out the Great Commission with signs and wonders following.

My goal in writing this book is not to propose new doctrines. Instead, we are embarking upon a quest to rediscover and resurrect eternal truths recorded in the Bible for centuries. We are endeavoring to revisit and reopen ancient wells of truth that have been filled up with traditions and doctrines of men through past years since that first church turned the world upside down.

Consider the wells Abraham dug that brought forth living water to nourish and satisfy his flocks, his herds and his family. They were stopped up by the Philistines in Genesis 26. These wells were not sabotaged by of an act of God; it was an enemy who stopped the flow of life-giving water.

The Philistines had one thought in mind. If they could stop the flow of water in the wells, they could successfully withhold something absolutely necessary to sustain life for Abraham's descendants. It's interesting to note that these wells are referred to in The King James Version of the Bible as "a well of springing [the margin reads *"living"* in the Hebrew language] water" (Genesis 26:19).

Jesus made a startling pronouncement concerning the coming ministry of the Holy Spirit. He said this in John's Gospel:

> ...If any man thirst, let him come unto me,
> and drink. He that believeth on me, as the
> scripture hath said, out of his belly [or spirit
> or innermost being] shall flow rivers of living
> water (John 7:37-38).

To ensure that in generations to come—including ours—this scripture would not become overly spiritualized and weakened of its clear meaning by Jesus, the next verse spells out the point in no uncertain terms precisely what Jesus meant:

> But this spake he of the Spirit, which they
> that believe on him should receive: for the
> Holy Ghost was not yet given; because that
> Jesus was not yet glorified (John 7:39).

The Master made it clear that those who would follow in His footsteps after He was raised from the dead and ascended into heaven could expect to receive a supernatural experience subsequent to salvation. Jesus said this experience would be so powerful He likened it to the force of many rivers flowing. This is nothing less than the power of the Holy Spirit abiding within and flowing out of Jesus' disciples.

It's important for us to note the setting in which these words were spoken by Jesus. Verses 37 through 39 took place during the middle of the Feast of Tabernacles. The scene opens on the last and greatest day of the feast, probably the seventh day. On this day the Torah (the Book of the Law) reading had concluded and the feast resumed. On this all-important seventh day, the priests led a procession carrying water drawn from the Pool of Siloam. They circled the altar seven times before pouring the water into the altar's funnels, where it flowed downward and eastward in the direction of the Red Sea.

This rite symbolized putting away the old by God and starting over again with all things being made new. It represented forgiveness of sins. The pouring of the water typified looking forward to a bountiful year of harvest brought about by abundant rainfall, preparing the ground for seedtime in the spring, and then helping to mature the grain for reaping in the autumn. In other words, it spoke of the former rains and the latter rains that were absolutely necessary for harvest.

Jesus chose this point during the feast to announce the coming of the Holy Spirit and His work of salvation and of empowering the believer for works of service or ministry. He clearly taught that "rivers of Living Water" was something every believer could expect to experience.

It's amazing to me that the one thing Jesus emphasized repeatedly that the Church should receive in order to fulfill the Great Commission is the one thing the Church has ignored and de-emphasized in our Christian experience. The clear and unmistakable directive from the Head of the Church was this: "Don't even *think* about preaching the gospel until you've been clothed with the same power of the Holy Spirit that clothed Me."

Unfortunately, many people have a mistaken notion about this clothing of the Spirit's power upon believers. I don't remember if it was something I heard preached as a young boy or if I simply reasoned it in my own mind, but like many others I had the misconception that Jesus performed mighty works during His earthly ministry *because* He was the Son of God. After all, if Jesus is the second person of the Godhead, co-equal in divine nature with God the Father, then certainly He ought to be able to do mighty, miraculous works. He's God, isn't He?

The answer to both these questions is a resounding yes. Jesus is God—God in a human body. He is the Word made flesh (John 1:14). Yet, so much of our thinking along certain lines of Jesus' ministry is simply incorrect. So many of our preconceived notions about the Master are things we've heard all our lives, but are not always supportable by the teaching of the scriptures. We need to carefully examine what we believe in the clear light of God's Word. Like the Berean believers, we need to search the scriptures diligently to determine whether or not the things we believe are accurate or not (Acts 17:11).

Truly, Jesus is our example in life and in ministry.

> ... leaving us an example, that ye should
> follow in his steps (Peter 2:21).

His life is the example of how we are to conduct our lives, how to allow the fruit of the Holy Spirit's presence in our lives to govern our relationships with others. Jesus is also an example of a life empowered by the Holy Spirit, thus enabling us to effectively minister to others.

If Jesus is our example, then we owe it to ourselves to study the scriptures carefully and prayerfully in order to learn all we can about what He did, and perhaps more importantly, *how* He did it. If Jesus expects the Church to continue what He started, then we must know something about the source of the power and ability behind the works He did.

Earlier, I spoke about the common misconception that miracles and healings occurred in the four Gospels simply because of Jesus' status as the Son of God. The reasoning goes something like this: If Jesus is God in the flesh, then as God He can do anything He wants by virtue of the fact that God is all-powerful, all-knowing and all-seeing. As sovereign God, He can do whatever He pleases, provided He does not violate His own Word.

> IF JESUS EXPECTS THE CHURCH TO CONTINUE WHAT HE STARTED, THEN WE MUST KNOW SOMETHING ABOUT THE SOURCE OF THE POWER AND ABILITY BEHIND THE WORKS HE DID.

After all, what kind of God would He be if He couldn't heal the sick, raise the dead and do the mighty miracles He did any time he wished, right? First, let's acknowledge something here. It's certainly true that God possesses all the divine attributes we just mentioned. There is none higher than God in rank, in authority, in wisdom, in power or in greatness.

Yet, in His sovereignty, He chose to become a man; He chose to become one of us. He was supernaturally conceived in the womb of a virgin. Jesus was the holy seed of the Word of God implanted in the womb of Mary by none other than the Holy Spirit. The same Holy Spirit who was poured out upon the 120 disciples in the Upper Room on the Day of Pentecost was the same Holy Spirit who hovered over the Virgin Mary overshadowing her and conceiving within her the holy child Jesus. The prophet Isaiah, hundreds of years before Christ's birth, called His name *Immanuel* meaning, *God with us.*

Jesus was God and man at the same time.

> For there is one God, and one mediator
> between God and men, the man Christ
> Jesus (Timothy 2:5).

Jesus did something absolutely remarkable—something so astounding the Church has never quite fully appreciated what He did. Before His incarnation on earth, Jesus voluntarily emptied Himself of His divine attributes. He chose to lay aside temporarily His God-form and freely relinquish the glory He had with God the Father *before* He came to be born in a stable in Bethlehem. This wonderful truth is taught in Paul's letter to the Church at Philippi.

The phrase in Philippians 2:7 reads *"... but made himself of no reputation ..."* The Greek language for this phrase is the word *kenao.* This word is defined in the following way: *to empty, to evacuate, to become nothing, to divest one's self of native dignity and power, to descend to an inferior position or condition.* I want to make it absolutely clear that this in no way means that Jesus at any time ever ceased being God. He is the God who dwells in eternity, meaning there never was a time when He wasn't God, and there never will be a time that He will not be God.

But He did let go for a time of the free use of His divine, godhead powers. Why did He do this? Among other things, Jesus was willing to do this in order to more fully identify with us and to provide a pattern for those of us who would choose to serve and follow Him. He did it to be a walking, talking example of what can be accomplished by us, His Church, in service to mankind.

If Jesus opened blind eyes based solely on the fact that He is the divine Son of God, then we would be forced to conclude that this would be something only God could do. If He made the lame to walk because He was God, then that certainly would leave the rest of us out.

Think with me for a moment. If what enabled Jesus to

perform the mighty works He did was based on His standing as the second person of the godhead, then why was it necessary for God to anoint Jesus with the Holy Ghost and with power?

> How God anointed Jesus of Nazareth with the Holy Ghost and with power: who went about doing good, and healing all that were oppressed of the devil; for God was with him (Acts 10:38).

GOOD QUESTION

If Jesus was already armed with all power, if He possessed all the divine attributes of God when He walked on the earth, why then would He need the addition of the Holy Spirit's anointing and power? There is but one compelling reason. Jesus emptied Himself of these qualities in order to become like one of us. He did it so He could be made like you and me in all things.

> Wherefore in all things it behooved him to be made like unto his brethren, that he might be a merciful and faithful high priest in things pertaining to God, to make reconciliation for the sins of the people (Hebrews 2:17).

Jesus made the decision to become a man who would be totally dependent upon God for all His needs to be met. He became totally reliant upon the Lord for the full empowerment of the Holy Spirit to equip Him for the work of the ministry.

Again, the book of Acts records a group of believers who obeyed Jesus' command to tarry or wait for the Holy Spirit to come upon them in power, enabling them to carry out their assignment. It's the same power Jesus received when He was baptized in the Jordan River by John the Baptist. It's no coincidence that Jesus did not perform a single miracle, open one blind eye, multiply any loaves and fishes or raise one person from the dead *until*

He came up out of the waters of baptism and the Holy Ghost descended upon Him in bodily form as a dove (Luke 3:22).

What was the source of Jesus' power? It was the baptism in the Holy Ghost. When Jesus stepped out of the water to embark upon His ministry to fast and pray and seek the face of God in the wilderness for 40 days and nights, He did so in the power and anointing of the Holy Ghost. Jesus lived in the power of the Holy Ghost every minute of every day until He drew His last breath on earth on the cross atop a hill called Calvary.

Now you can begin to understand why Jesus was so insistent that His followers receive this same experience called the baptism in the Holy Spirit. Jesus knew it would take more than human wisdom, human reasoning and mere intellectual prowess to draw people into the kingdom of God. He knew it would require preaching energized by the Holy Spirit to cause the Word to penetrate the hearts of men and women and not simply to challenge their minds.

We are not called to debate people into the kingdom of God. We are not to use scare tactics to save people from hell and get them into heaven. We are not expected to employ lofty, intellectual arguments to persuade people to receive eternal life.

If anyone had the ability to use the advanced wisdom and learning of man to drive home the truths of the gospel, surely it would have been Paul the apostle. Educated in the prestigious school of Gamaliel, he was one of the most gifted and learned Hebrew students in all of Israel. Saul of Tarsus (later known as Paul) was a master pupil of the Jewish religion.

But in the final analysis, Paul did not rely upon his religious pedigree or his great learning or intellectual accomplishments to aid him in propagating the glorious gospel. Despite the fact that he had diligently labored to attain all these things, Paul said that when he came to the Corinthians to bring them the gospel he did not do so with "excellency of speech or wisdom" (1 Corinthians 2:1). Instead, he determined that his speech and his preaching be not with enticing words of man's wisdom, but rather with the power and demonstration of the Holy Spirit (1 Corinthians 2:4-5).

In other words, Paul preached the Word of God with an entire dependency upon God to confirm or back up the Word He preached with signs and wonders by the power of the Holy Spirit. These fearless men and women in Acts were unlearned in the ways of formal religious training. But they displayed a boldness and a power that was *not* of this world. Heaven backed them up. Jesus showed up when they preached—not in His own physical body per se, but in the power of the Holy Spirit.

The Christians in Acts did not simply sit in their pews (they didn't have any!) and listen to a preacher deliver a sermon. They didn't leave the church building, shake the preacher's hand and compliment him on the great sermon he just preached. They didn't return to their homes, go to work the next day and then return to the church building on Wednesday night to hear another sermon, only to repeat the cycle all over again. That was definitely not the program of the early church.

God moved through the believers outside the church building. There's certainly nothing wrong with meeting in a building for fellowship, hearing the Word preached, worshiping God with our tithes and offerings, praying for one another, and being encouraged in the things of God. But if that is the extent of our ministry as a church, we are missing it big time.

Why do I say that? I say so because the pattern, the model of the Church, already has been established for us in Acts, the founding document of the Church. Those disciples understood that ministry should take place *outside* the walls of the meeting place. They understood also that ministry was not just the responsibility of a professional clergy.

Their concept of the Church, given them by Jesus, was that of a Holy Spirit-empowered redeemed band of believers alert to opportunities to take a Living Christ into the lives of hurting people. Having done that, they fully expected a demonstration of God's mercy and power to pour into the lives of those being ministered to in a very tangible way.

In many of our King James authorized versions of the Bible the first page of Acts reads something like this: "The Acts of the Apostles." For years I never gave this wording much thought until I began to actually read and study Acts. I discovered it wasn't simply the apostles God used to spearhead the activities of the new church. It wasn't just Peter, Paul and other apostles alone who were used by the Lord to perform mighty deeds in this great historical narrative that chronicles the activities of the first church. It is true that much of the story of Acts centers around the ministry of Peter in the first segment of the book. Then beginning with Chapter 13, the focus shifts to the ministry exploits of Paul. But these two were by no means the only people God used to write the great chapters of the glorious works of this wonderful living organism called the Church. In fact, Acts did not end at Chapter 28. You will notice there is not a benediction at the close of this book as there is in many other books of the New Testament. The fact is, believers are still writing chapters in the book of Acts today.

For instance, in Chapter 6 we read that Stephen, full of faith and power, did great wonders and miracles among the people. Yet, we should note that Stephen was *not* an apostle. He was not one of the original 12 handpicked by Jesus to be one of His successors in ministry. Stephen was what we would refer to today as a deacon in the church. He, along with seven others, was selected to serve the basic needs of the people who made up the church. Would to God we would have deacons in our churches today who possess the same qualities Stephen did—men full of faith, full of power, full of wisdom and full of the Holy Ghost!

Philip was another man chosen to serve as a deacon. Yet, speaking of Philip, the Bible says,

> Then Philip went down to the city of
> Samaria, and preached Christ unto them.
> And the people with one accord gave
> heed unto those things which Philip spake,
> hearing and seeing the miracles which he did
> (Acts 8:5-6).

Many were saved and many miracles occurred. And Philip was a deacon, not an apostle!

The Bible also records the example of Ananias, whom God used in a mighty way. Like Stephen and Philip before him, Ananias also did not claim the distinction of serving as an apostle in the church. Scriptures refer to him simply as, *"a certain disciple."* His only claim to fame, the thing that qualified him to be used by God to minister in the church, was the fact that he was a disciple of Jesus Christ. God used him to lay hands on Paul (then Saul of Tarsus) to fill him with the Holy Ghost and restore his eyesight.

So we can readily see that the pattern already has been established for the work of the Church; the foundation already has been laid. The divine pattern is repeated throughout the book of Acts. Every chapter seems to throb with the supernatural. God used common, ordinary people with all their flaws and imperfections, and molded them into a mighty vanguard of evangelism, healing and deliverance.

My friends, that is the gospel in a nutshell. That is our task. That is our commission. That is our calling. That's why we're here. It's time for us to stop merely going to church. It's time for us to start *being* the Church. It's time for us to begin doing the same works they did. It's time for us to preach the same gospel anointed with the same Holy Spirit and lift up the same Jesus as did the believers in the book of Acts. THE TIME IS NOW!

66

I AGREE

There's no need to reinvent the Church to fit 21st century standards and culture. God got it right the first time! His concept of what the Church should be and how it should function already has proven to be successful. The blueprint for the building and equipping of Christ's body on the earth already has been drawn by the hand of the Master Draftsman. By all means, we should use the technological tools, social media communication and contemporary resources available today to broaden and advance the message of the gospel. As long as the core message of Jesus Christ is being communicated to people who haven't yet heard it, let's make use of every means at our disposal to preach Jesus.

Yet, here is the question we must address: Do we have what it takes to humble ourselves, take a fresh, unbiased view of Acts and be willing to walk in the same fearless faith as those early disciples of Christ? Are we willing to adopt a radical mindset about furthering the claims of the gospel to folks all around us like they did? Or, will we be content to languish in our safe, comfortable Christian anonymity, blending into the culture of the day, being careful not to rock the boat while we stay huddled inside the safety of our churches, wiling away the time until Jesus comes to rescue us from this world?

GOOD QUESTIONS. SOMETHING TO THINK ABOUT REFLECT UPON

Friends, if we are really honest with ourselves and admit that this pretty much describes our approach to the Christian faith today, then we need to repent before God. We need to be willing to turn from such a weak, timid concept of Christianity that hides the power of God and the reality of a risen and glorified Savior from folks who need to hear the Good News the most.

Several years ago, Alex Haley wrote a best-selling book titled *Roots*. It later became an award- winning television mini-series that told the story of a race of people literally tracing their roots. These people, who were hungry to learn of their past, asked the questions:

- What is my bloodline?
- What is my heritage?
- Where did I come from?
- Who were my forbears?

Interestingly enough, these are the same questions we ought to be asking in the Church world today. We ought to be willing to go back in time, past all the present-day sectarian, denominational groups and discover our roots. And in doing so, we should ask: Where did we come from? What did we look like in the beginning? What is our heritage? What did we do in the beginning?

In order for these probing questions to be adequately answered, we must move away from the contemporary church world, away from all the various denominations that make up the Church today and return to the pattern established in the Book of Acts. In Acts we find a 28-chapter blueprint of what the Church looked like in the very beginning

You see, friend, how the Church looked in its conception is *exactly* how it should look today. Every individual church should have what they had in the Acts church. From the throne of God there flowed into that church salvation, deliverance, signs and wonders, divine healing and the ministry of angels. It is God's plan that in this dark hour of human history that we have all the supernatural power of God's Spirit, all the ministry of angels, all the help we need in order to prevail against and overcome the dark forces at work in our world today.

It's time to get back to our roots in the Book of Acts. God is waiting for a generation of believers who will allow the Holy Spirit to have His way in their lives and be believers through whom He can once again flow forth as rivers of living water.

Let's determine to be that generation.

CHAPTER 3

THE HOLY SPIRIT:
CEO OF THE CHURCH

The supreme task of the Church is world evangelization. Our assignment is to carry Jesus' final words to the ends of the earth so every creature can benefit from the message of reconciliation. When we understand the awesome price that was required and freely paid by Jesus to liberate men and women from sin and the effects of spiritual death, we will be compelled to take the news of the finished work of the cross to the nations with a fierce determination.

When we take our place as messengers and announce by word and deed the good news of a living Christ to suffering humanity, several wonderful things take place. First of all, we exert kingdom influence on the earth. This is important. Jesus Himself preached the gospel of the kingdom throughout the four Gospels and ministered extensively on the subject of the kingdom of God. In doing so, He let people know that in the midst of an earthly kingdom all around us, there exists an invisible, supernatural realm or kingdom not of this world. It's a kingdom ruled by God; a kingdom with no earthly limitations or imperfections.

Jesus spoke of a kingdom where God rules and reigns according to absolute righteousness, justice and peace that surpasses our feeble human understanding. As Christians we enter into and dwell in this kingdom while at the same time living natural lives here on the earth. Moreover, since God is King of His Kingdom and possesses absolute right of rulership in it, His Word has become the law of the kingdom. Whatever He decrees is the way it is in His kingdom.

The Bible says that where there is word of a king there is power (Ecclesiastes 8:4). There is power in God's kingdom to set you free from the chains of sin and oppression. There's power to be transformed into a brand-new person, power to think in totally new ways—to think like God thinks. There's power to forgive those who've wronged you and experience liberation from the deadly poison of unforgiveness. There's power to heal your body and your emotions, and there's power that enables you to maintain a continual, abiding fellowship with God and experience the manifestation of the Holy Spirit in your life.

But something else takes place as we begin to share this great gospel message with others—persecution. Persecutions and afflictions will come our way as we deliver a message that runs counter not only to the culture all around us, but also to the prevailing religious status quo. We can be sure that when our Christian lives and experiences begin to match those of believers in the first century Church, many around us won't be happy about it.

In the same way that believers in the early church were derided by the religious leaders for spreading a new doctrine throughout Jerusalem that conflicted with Orthodox Judaism, you can be sure the religious establishment today will not embrace the new work of the Holy Spirit God is performing in the Church today. Frankly, many people you know will not be breathlessly waiting to embrace this new dimension of God's presence and power of the Holy Spirit that many in our day have received.

But if we keep in mind that we are Christ's ambassadors sent forth to represent Him on the earth and endeavor to maintain a sweet spirit, we will succeed in our task. Keeping a sweet spirit may not be easy, but it is vitally important. In order to truly walk as an ambassador of Christ, we must be patient and kind with those who oppose us, thereby enabling the Holy Spirit to convict people of their need of all that Jesus has to offer them. The world should see what we have and want it. They *need* what we have. They just don't know it yet because, for the most part, people have been religiously brainwashed instead of New Testament taught and trained.

The Holy Spirit coming upon believers in power is not really new at all. It is well more than 2,000 years old. It started with the birth of the Church, and God has never withdrawn this holy experience from the Church. At some point after the first century church exploded on the scene in Jerusalem, church leaders decided that their own ideas were superior to God's. Unfortunately, many agreed that an enduement of power from heaven was somehow no longer necessary and, in fact, had passed away.

Sometime after the third century, official titles, prominent positions, political influence and a highly organized religious hierarchy led to what has been called the Dark Ages in the Church. It was so called because the light of God's Word was snuffed out and replaced with ecclesiastical doctrines of men with no power to save, heal or set men free from their sins.

Out of the Dark Ages came the great politico-religious, ecclesiastical Roman hierarchy, which in time dominated the whole world, both political and religious.

> And the same condition has developed out
> of every fallen movement. An illegitimate,
> hybrid monster has come forth.[1]

Yet when those 120 Holy Ghost-baptized firebrands exited the Upper Room on the Day of Pentecost, they stepped out fresh from the manifest presence of God, fully in love with Jesus, filled with the fruits and gifts of the Holy Spirit and possessing a 100 percent consecration to God. That was the secret of the success of this first church. They were completely sold out to God, and God was sold out to the Church.

I'm convinced that today's church will never be fully successful in carrying out Christ's mandate of the Great Commission if we fail to allow the Holy Spirit to have His rightful place in the ministry of the Church today. We will fail miserably in confronting and challenging the religious status quo of the day. Furthermore, we will not be the light of the world and the salt of the earth that Jesus said we should be if the Holy Spirit is not permitted to regain His rightful position as chief executive officer, or CEO, of the Church today.

After all, an organization's CEO plays an extremely important role in the overall success of a company. He or she is charged with the responsibility of the day-to-day operations, the failure or success, the profit or loss, and the growth or the decline of the fortunes of the enterprise. The skills, expertise and leadership ability of the CEO are what makes or breaks an organization.

CEOs do just exactly what their title implies—they *execute.* They make things happen. They get things done. The president of the United States occupies what our founding fathers termed the executive branch of our federal government. Executives are responsible for carrying out the policies of the company and for the general oversight of the business they have been appointed to administrate.

THIS IS SO TRUE
BELIEVE THIS IS A HANGING TODAY

In God's economy, the Holy Spirit has been designated by God to be the member of the Holy Trinity responsible for executing, or carrying out, God's plan on the earth. But He does it through the Church. So then it's surprising how little the average Christian knows about this divine personality, the Holy Spirit.

I can attest to this in my own life. As a young boy growing up and going to Church, I didn't have the faintest notion of who the Holy Spirit was. In the Methodist Church I attended in eastern Ohio, we would close our Sunday services by singing a hymn of praise called the Doxology. Maybe you remember the words of this age-old hymn:

> Praise God from whom all blessings flow.
> Praise Him all creatures here below.
> Praise Him above, ye heavenly hosts.
> Praise Father, Son and Holy Ghost.

In my youth and limited understanding of spiritual things, I thought our congregation was singing, *"Praise Him all preachers here below."* For a long time I thought only preachers could praise the Lord. I learned later on that all of God's creatures are exhorted to offer praise and worship to God, which includes you and me. Nevertheless, even though the Doxology mentioned the Holy Ghost, I really had no idea what that meant. I had seen enough horror movies at the local movie theater in my hometown to know that I wanted to run as far away from a ghost as my young legs would carry me.

Still, a part of me reasoned that if we were giving homage and praise to the Holy Ghost in our little Methodist church, then He couldn't be all that bad. After all, He is the *Holy* Ghost. There must be something about Him that sets Him apart from all other ghosts. Years later I discovered that the King James Bible, which was translated out of the original languages into English in 1611, was laced with Shakespearean idioms and phrases that were in common use in early 17th century in England. The name *Holy Ghost* means, of course, Holy Spirit.

As I grew in my understanding of the things of God, I began to learn some things about the nature, the personhood and the qualities of the Holy Spirit. I discovered, for example, the triune nature of God. I learned that God is one eternal deity, yet He manifests Himself in three divine personalities: God the Father, God the Son and God the Holy Ghost. I further learned that although the word *trinity* does not appear in the Bible, the concept of the union and interaction between these three divine personalities is revealed in many places in scripture.

Even in my younger years, I knew some things about God. I would have been quick to point out that God is the Creator. I knew that God formed and fashioned man in His own image and likeness, created the planets and all life on earth, and that somehow He holds all things together in order to maintain order in the universe.

I also knew something about Jesus. I knew He was God's only begotten Son born in a manger in Bethlehem. I knew He grew up and lived for 33½ years, and for three years He preached and taught and healed people. Then on the last day of His life on the earth, He died on a Roman cross outside the city walls of Jerusalem. I understood that Jesus died for the sins of the world. I learned from my Methodist Sunday school teacher, who happened to be my dad, that if you believe in Jesus and invite Him into your heart, He will give you eternal life and make you a child of God.

Later on, however, I came to realize that perhaps no doctrine of the Christian faith has been so misunderstood, so neglected and so inaccurately taught in the Church than the person and the work of the Holy Spirit. This is especially true when it comes to His role in present-day ministry.

The scriptures declare Him to be the revealer of *all* truth, the active agent behind all the works of redemption. It is *in* the Spirit *by* the Spirit and *through* the Spirit that we are saved and baptized into the body of Christ. All the works of conviction, repentance, regeneration and illumination—as well as the work of sanctification or holiness—come to us by the agency of the Holy Spirit.

But one additional work of the Holy Spirit stands out as the most neglected aspect of His ministry. When asked in faith, He fills believers with His presence and power in a particular work that the Bible refers to as a *baptism*. It is a complete immersion of His being into ours. This mighty Holy Spirit is the source and the supply of wisdom, guidance and power to the Church. He directs, energizes and empowers the Church in its ministry of presenting Christ to the world.

I want to share with you a quote from the late Samuel Chadwick, who was for many years the principal of Cliff College in Sheffield, England. Chadwick wrote a book in 1933 titled *The Way to Pentecost*. The following quote is taken from a chapter in his book titled "The Church Without the Spirit":

> The work of the Spirit in the Church is set forth in the promises of Jesus on the eve of His departure, and demonstrated in the Acts of the Apostles. The Gospels tell of, "all that Jesus began to do and to teach, until the day in which He was taken up," and the Acts of the Apostles tell of all that He continued to do and teach after the day in which He was received up.
>
> The Holy Spirit is the active, administrative Agent of the glorified Son. He is the Paraclete, the Deputy, the acting Representative of the ascended Christ. His mission is to glorify Christ by perpetuating His character, establishing His Kingdom, and accomplishing His redeeming purpose in the world.
>
> The Church is the Body of Christ, and the Spirit is the Spirit of Christ. He fills the Body, directs

its movements, controls its Members, inspires its wisdom, and supplies its strength. He guides into truth, sanctifies its agents, and empowers for witnessing. The work of the Church is to minister the Spirit, to speak His message, and transmit His power.

The Spirit has never abdicated His authority nor relegated His power. Neither Pope nor Parliament, neither Conference, nor Council is supreme in the Church of Christ. The Church that is man-managed instead of God-governed is doomed to failure. A ministry that is College-trained but not Spirit-filled works no miracles. The Church that multiplies committees and neglects prayer may be fussy, noisy and enterprising but it labours in vain and spends itself for naught.

It is possible to excel in mechanics and fail in dynamics. There is a superabundance of machinery; what is wanting is Power. To run an organization needs no God. Man can supply the energy, enterprise, and enthusiasm for things human. The real work of the Church depends upon the power of the Spirit.[2]

The church we read of in Acts, a church actively involved in carrying out Christ's assignment to preach the gospel to every creature, was a Church born of the Spirit, empowered by the Spirit, filled with the Spirit and led in all its activities by the Spirit. In fact, if you compare the lofty place the Holy Spirit held in the early church with His nearly nonexistent ministry in today's church, the contrast between the two is startling.

You cannot read the book of Acts and compare the works of the early church with today's church without becoming aware that something is missing. A certain vitality and energy is noticeably absent in contemporary Christian practice and experience. If you're honest, you simply cannot study the chronicles of the first century church without quickly recognizing that we are being terribly short-changed in our modern Christian experience.

When we read through the pages of Acts, it's important that we not relegate the book to simply that of a historical narrative of the early church. Instead, when we read through this wonderful book, we should do so with the same interest that we do when we read a newspaper article or view a cable news channel broadcasting a breaking news story. We should be absorbed and riveted. When we pore over its pages, we should come away with the notion that *we* today should be used by the Holy Spirit to accomplish the same things and more. The book of Acts is not simply an account of what the first century church accomplished; it's the prescription for an ailing 21st century church.

EARLY BELIEVERS DID NOT SIMPLY PREACH ABOUT JESUS; THEY DID THE SAME WORKS HE DID.

Early believers did not simply preach about Jesus; they did the same works He did. They did not merely offer an explanation of the gospel; rather, they were empowered to demonstrate it. In other words, they showed how it worked; they proved how it worked. And as they preached in the power of Jesus' name, the Holy Spirit *confirmed* their words with signs, wonders and miracles.

What was the secret of their success? Did they have a bigger God than we do? Of course not. Did they have a better Bible than us? No, in fact the New Testament hadn't even been written at that time. Was the Holy Spirit more powerful in those days than He is now? Absolutely not.

I don't believe for a moment that God intended there be a powerful, world-changing, mighty Church 2,000 years ago, but today He's willing to settle for a weak, powerless, compromising and largely ineffective Church. God never changes. Jesus never changes. The Holy Spirit never changes. Period. We are the ones who have changed. At some point in church history, believers decided to place more confidence in the theories of men than in the truth of God's Word.

Through the centuries, doctrines and traditions of men have superseded truth that is clearly taught in the Bible. Instead of heeding Paul's instructions to "rightly divide the Word of truth," too many people have believed the words of unwise theologians who took denominational scissors to the pages of the Bible and removed verses that didn't agree with their particular view of doctrine.

The church in Acts placed a much greater premium on the ministry of the Holy Spirit than the Church today. Those early believers understood that they needed to possess the same supernatural equipping that empowered Jesus Himself when He was here. God so loved the world that He gave Jesus to pay the ransom note the devil held against the sins of fallen humanity. But God had another gift He wanted His children to possess.

The Holy Spirit is God's gift—not to the world—but to the Church. In the Gospel of John, Chapters 14, 15 and 16, Jesus taught the disciples extensively on the coming ministry of the Holy Spirit. Four times in the Gospel of Luke, and in Acts, the Holy Spirit is referred to as *"the promise of the Father."*

More to the point, Jesus commanded His disciples in Luke 24:49 and in Acts 1:4 to wait for the enduement or the baptism of the Holy Spirit. What right do we have to change a commandment of the Lord into an option? To *command* is defined in the dictionary in the following way: *"the formal exercise of absolute authority as by a sovereign, or military leader, to direct with authority; to have authority or jurisdiction over."* [3]

By virtue of His conquest over Satan and His subsequent crowning of all authority and power in heaven and in earth, Jesus has been placed into sovereign rulership over the Church that He purchased with His own blood. It is His Church! And He reserves the God-granted right to issue whatever official orders and decrees He feels necessary for the proper equipping and arming of His body of believers. We have received orders from headquarters. Jesus, our commander-in-chief, has given us a job to do.

He already has fought the battle and won a great victory over our adversary the devil. And it was the Holy Spirit who gave Jesus the power and the wisdom to defeat these hosts of hell at every turn during His earthly ministry. Jesus understood that we cannot prevail against the supernatural strategies of our sinister opponent by relying upon human wisdom and strength alone. It takes the supernatural power of the Holy Ghost in a believer's life to enable us to enforce the devil's defeat that Jesus won for us by means of His death, burial and triumphant resurrection.

How the devil must laugh at our puny attempts to replace the Lord's supernatural armor, weapons and power of the Holy Spirit with our denominational doctrines and our petty bickering over whether the baptism of the Holy Spirit and speaking with other tongues is still a viable and normal part of Christian experience today.

We cannot debate people into the kingdom of God or merely appeal to their sense of logic and reason. It's not by meeting physical needs only that causes people to want to know Jesus as Savior. But once a person comes into contact with the power of the Holy Spirit like those in the early church—once they witness God's manifest presence—they will know that God is real.

When blind eyes are opened, when the deaf can suddenly hear and the crippled can walk, then the world will know God is real. When the Holy Spirit removes the scales from people's eyes and enables them to "see" Jesus nailed to a cross in order to pay the penalty for their sins, then people will come to Him. And they will come by the multitudes. The last thing we need today is more religion. We don't need motivational speeches disguised as sermons by TV preachers telling us how to "feel right." We need Spirit-anointed preaching that teaches us how to "be right."

People don't need opinions and theories. They need the same New Testament experience that the 120 believers received in the Upper Room on the Day of Pentecost. They need the rushing, mighty wind and fire of the Holy Spirit sent from heaven into their lives. They need an encounter with the Comforter, the Paraclete, the divine Helper, the Spirit of God.

Jesus said, "You shall receive power after that the Holy Spirit is come upon you" (Acts 1:8). The same Holy Spirit who clothed Jesus with supernatural ability and power and caused people to be astonished by His teaching. It's the same power that enabled Jesus to heal the sick, raise the dead, give sight to blind eyes and cleanse people afflicted with flesh-destroying leprosy. Now this Holy Spirit stands ready to clothe *you*. Amazing.

Again, it's ironic to me that the one issue Jesus adamantly emphasized as a major principle in starting and maintaining the Church, is the one thing the Church has neglected the most: the absolute necessity of the baptism in the Holy Spirit in the believer's life. No other single Bible truth has been more downplayed, ignored or neglected as this all-important one. Various Christian sects have endeavored to explain it away and persuade believers they've already received all of the Holy Spirit that is available when they got saved. But nothing could be further from the truth. Power awaits you my friend.

It is a scriptural fact that when you were born again, you received a work of the Holy Spirit.

> But ye are not in the flesh, but in the Spirit,
> if so be that the Spirit of God dwell in you.
> Now if any man have not the Spirit of Christ,
> he is none of his (Romans 8:9).

At the moment of the New Birth, the Spirit of God comes to make His home in the heart of the believer. That's when our bodies become what Paul called "temples of the Holy Ghost" (1

Corinthians 6:19). When we yield to the Holy Spirit's drawing us toward God's gift of eternal life in Christ Jesus, we experience a work of the Spirit called regeneration or spiritual rebirth. We received the power to become the sons of God and new creatures in Christ Jesus.

But there's more—so much more! The Bible clearly teaches that there is yet another measure of the Holy Spirit's impartation we can receive. Christians are not only *born* of the Spirit, but they can also be *filled* with the Spirit.

It's not a question of, "Well, I already got the Holy Spirit when I got saved." The issue every Christian needs to settle is this: "Am I willing to yield more fully to God's Word and His will for my life?" Do you hunger for more of God? Is there a yearning and a stirring within you to be absolutely consumed with God's presence in your life?

Multiplied thousands of believers in churches around the world love Jesus, go to church, support the work of the church with their tithes and offerings, and yet they are struggling. Their Christian experience has become a monotonous routine of plodding along in denominational emptiness and frustration. My heart goes out to pastors attempting to lead their congregations and help folks in their quest for spiritual growth and development based solely on what they've been taught in seminaries and theology classes.

Many churches today are flatlining; there's barely a pulse left. Why? Because the majority of churches in America are not empowered and energized by the Holy Spirit, but instead are being controlled by a religious hierarchy holding sway over them. If many pastors and church leaders were totally honest, they would admit they are miserable and ready to quit. While they desperately buy into current church growth formulas and try out the latest gimmicks to stimulate church attendance, many grow more dissatisfied and discouraged in their hearts. Deep inside they yearn for an intimate walk with the Master and a powerful, satisfying Christian experience.

It's interesting in Acts 19 that when Paul, in the course of his ministry travels, went to Ephesus he encountered disciples of John the Baptist there. Notice that the first thing he inquired of them was whether or not they had received the Holy Spirit.

> And it came to pass, that, while Apollos was at Corinth, Paul having passed through the upper coasts came to Ephesus; and finding certain disciples, He said unto them, Have ye received the Holy Ghost since ye believed? And they said unto him, We have not so much as heard whether there be any Holy Ghost. And he said unto them, Unto what then were ye baptized? And they said, Unto John's baptism. Then Paul said, John verily baptized with the baptism of repentance, saying unto the people, that they should believe on him which should come after him, that is, on Christ Jesus. When they heard this, they were baptized in the name of the Lord Jesus. And when Paul had laid his hands on them, the Holy Ghost came on them and they spoke with tongues and prophesied. And all the men were about twelve (Acts 19:1-7).

It's important to note that these 12 men Paul encountered were Christians. They were disciples of John the Baptist, who earlier had shared with them that there was One coming who was mightier than he was. These 12 believed John's preaching about Jesus and received Him as savior even though they never saw Jesus in person or heard Him preach.

Consider the following informative explanation in the *Full Life Bible Commentary to the New Testament* referring to these verses in Acts 19:

> Some interpreters contend that the
> description of the twelve as "some" (or
> certain) disciples indicates that they
> did not belong to the Christian group at
> Ephesus but were rather a group of John
> the Baptist's disciples... the Book of Acts,
> however, fails to support the view that
> passes the twelve off as being completely
> distinct and separate from the Christian
> community.

Luke consistently uses the word *disciples*, which in the Greek is *mathetai and* refers to Christians (Acts 6:1,7; 9:1,19,26; 11:26; 14:21-22). Luke also uses the same pronoun in three passages to refer to known Christians Ananias (9:10), Tabitha (9:36) and Timothy (16:1). Whether singular or plural, this indefinite pronoun describes the followers of Christ. "These twelve men were pre-Pentecostal Christians. They were converted, but not filled with the Spirit." [4]

These disciples in Ephesus were clearly believers in Jesus Christ. They were born again by the Holy Spirit, but had not yet heard about the *baptism* of the Holy Spirit.

Consider with me also the following passage from *Word Studies in the New Testament* by Marvin R. Vincent, D.D., commenting on Acts 19:1:

> ... [These were] disciples of John the
> Baptist, who, like Apollos, had been
> instructed and baptized by the followers of
> the Baptist, and had joined the fellowship
> of Christians ... there was something which
> drew the attention of the Apostle (Paul)
> immediately upon his arrival. They lacked,
> apparently, some of the tokens of the
> higher life that pervaded the nascent [the
> newly developed] church; they were devout,
> rigorous, austere, but were wanting in the

joy, the radiancy, the enthusiasm which
were conspicuous in others.[5]

When Paul encountered these believers in Ephesus, he did
not ask them, "Since you've believed on Jesus, I'm interested to
know your opinion about the baptism in the Holy Spirit." Paul
could not have cared less about their opinion of the ministry
of the Holy Spirit. Instead, Paul came right to the point. He
accurately perceived that something vital was missing in their
Christian experience, and he ministered to them what was
missing. Scripture records that when Paul laid hands on them,
they spoke in tongues and prophesied.

> What the scripture says concerning the
> Holy Spirit is one thing, but what some man,
> men, or whole denominations may think
> is often miles away from the truth. Whole
> denominations, creeds and doctrines have
> been built up and are being fostered on what
> some man or men think about the Holy Spirit.
> On the other hand, whole denominations,
> churches, and thousands of hungry people
> are being deprived of what God wishes to
> give them and what their souls are hungry
> for, because those who are in power and
> have rule over them, in their soul-destroying
> ignorance, profess to be wise. "My people
> are destroyed for lack of knowledge" (Hosea
> 4:6). How glaringly true in this case, but woe
> unto them thru whom the perishing comes.[6]

The truth is, we need a Bible experience of the baptism in the
Holy Spirit, complete with the Bible evidence of having received
that wonderful experience. Jesus did not even begin His ministry,
perform one single miracle or cast out any evil spirits until He
stepped out of the River Jordan full of the Holy Ghost and power.
That is when the Spirit of God descended upon Him in bodily form
as a dove. This was the Master's personal empowerment with the

Holy Spirit, equipping Him for the ministry that awaited Him.

Jesus was totally dependent upon God for what He accomplished in ministry. He said, "I only do what I see my Father do, and I only say what I hear my Father say" (John 5:19 and John 12:49). In other words, it was God through the Holy Spirit guiding and directing Jesus in His preaching, teaching and healing the sick. It's important for us to appreciate that if Jesus—our great High Priest, the Captain of our salvation, and our soon coming King of Kings and Lord of Lords—placed that level of esteem, honor and total dependency upon the Holy Spirit, how much more should we?

Nothing can take the place of the Holy Spirit in your life—not years of seminary training, not acquiring multiple and advanced theological degrees, and not the benefit of possessing a dynamic, charismatic personality. None of these can ever take the place of the life-giving power and anointing of the Holy Spirit sent to the Church from heaven.

Rev. B. H. Clendennen, an ordained minister with the Assemblies of God for more than 50 years and pioneer of the School of Christ International, offers the following observation:

> It is my personal conviction that the
> message of Pentecost is God the Father,
> through God the Holy Ghost, displaying
> God the Son, through the vehicle called the
> Church. [7]

People who suffer today from blindness aren't interested in a Jesus who once opened blind eyes 2,000 years ago. Instead, they desperately need the healing and miracle working power of a Jesus who is still interested in restoring sight to the blind. Deaf folks aren't thrilled to read in their Bibles of a Jesus who used to restore hearing to people 2,000 years ago. When blind and deaf folks read these glorious accounts of Jesus healing people, how their hearts must cry out, *"Lord Jesus, you did it for them, won't you do it for me?"* People who feel buried beneath a load of depression, anxiety and fears are not thrilled to hear of a Jesus who used to heal the brokenhearted and bring deliverance to the captives. No, they need His help today, and thank God Jesus still delivers those in need.

Throughout the Word of God, Jesus was everywhere moved with compassion toward suffering humanity. He didn't simply feel sorry for them, and He certainly didn't ignore them. The Bible says Jesus is "touched with the feeling of our infirmities" (Hebrews 4:15). What does that mean? It means that when He ministered to the man at the Pool of Bethesda in Jerusalem— when He spat on the ground and made clay of the spittle and rubbed the clay into the blind man's eyes, two things were happening.

First, because Jesus was moved with compassion, that means He suffered with the afflicted man. That's what the word *compassion* means: *"to suffer with another."* I believe Jesus entered into the blind man's condition. He felt the pitch black of night that the blind man felt every day of his life when He touched his eyes. I believe for a brief moment Jesus took on the man's affliction, fully relating to the feelings of hopelessness and despair of one suffering with blindness.

Secondly, because Jesus only did what He saw His Father do (John 5:19), He acted out in the physical realm what He saw His Father do in the spirit realm. Making clay of the spittle and rubbing the mixture on the man's unseeing eyes was certainly not the method Jesus used to heal every blind person. He used a variety of means and methods to bring healing to the sick, and they worked because the Bible says, "How God anointed Jesus of Nazareth with the Holy Ghost and with power, who went about doing good, and healing all that were oppressed of the devil; for God was with him" (Acts 10:38).

In the same way Jesus was sent by God to ransom lost humanity, we also are sent by God to minister to a darkened, hell-bound, demon-ridden, sickness-infested world, but not in our own power or wisdom. Its God's power in us that is sufficient alone to set the captives free. The Holy Ghost empowers Christ's Church today as He empowered Jesus during His

> THE HOLY GHOST EMPOWERS CHRIST'S CHURCH TODAY AS HE EMPOWERED JESUS DURING HIS EARTHLY MINISTRY— POWER TO DO, POWER TO BE, POWER TO RECEIVE, POWER TO TRANSMIT, POWER TO HEAL, POWER TO SPEAK, POWER TO STAND AND POWER TO WITNESS.

earthly ministry—power to do, power to be, power to receive, power to transmit, power to heal, power to speak, power to stand and power to witness.

May the Church today be set free once and for all from the man-made shackles of tradition and sectarianism that we've substituted in place of truth that makes men free! The lost need to be saved. The sick need to be healed. The empty need to be filled. The oppressed and possessed need to be delivered.

Time is flying and men and women are dying. The harvest is waiting to be reaped, and to accomplish the task, the Church must have the power of the Holy Ghost. Moses could have done little or nothing in Pharaoh's court in Egypt without mighty signs and wonders sent from heaven to back him up. Likewise, the Church cannot accomplish its task without supernatural manifestations from heaven.

Friend, this is what it all comes down to in reality. The Holy Spirit has been here for time and eternity. He was active and very much involved in every aspect of creation. From Genesis through Revelation, God's Holy Spirit is noticeably at work. At the very moment of creation in Genesis, the Holy Spirit, the breath of God Himself, was waiting to take the command of God, "Let there be light" and transform God's spoken word into action—into tangible, visible and touchable life. Consider this verse from Genesis in several translations.

> And the Spirit of God moved upon the face of the waters (Genesis 1:2).

> ... while a mighty wind swept over the waters (NAB).

> ...the Spirit of God was hovering over the surface of the waters (NLT).

> ...the Spirit of God was moving (hovering, brooding) over the face of the waters (AMP).

In the same way that the Holy Spirit was and is God's CEO, who acted on God's command to bring forth light, divide the waters and create all life on planet Earth, this CEO also created the Church. The Holy Spirit was not only active in the birth of the Church, He also carries out the full administration of its ministry.

In His farewell address to His disciples on the night before He was betrayed, Jesus prepared His disciples for the coming ministry of the Holy Spirit. Explaining how necessary and important the Holy Spirit's ministry would be, Jesus said, "It is expedient for you that I go away; for if I go not away, the Comforter will not come unto you; but if I go, I will send him unto you" (John 16:7).

The work the Holy Spirit was to perform in the Church was so vital that Jesus was not only willing to depart, Jesus <u>had</u> to go away in order to make a way for the fullness of the Spirit's ministry on earth. The work of the Holy Spirit could not be done by any other. More importantly, if His work was left undone, then all of Jesus' miracles and teachings—the whole purpose of

Jesus' incarnation—could not be properly understood, much less received and enjoyed.

I realize these are sweeping statements. But they are not my opinions. Neither are they the theories of other people. These statements about the absolute necessity of the Spirit's work are Jesus' very own words.

> Howbeit when he, the Spirit of truth, is come, he will guide you into all truth. He shall glorify me: for he shall receive of mine, and shall shew it unto you (John 16:13-14).

Notice that Jesus refers to the Holy Spirit as the Spirit of truth. Earlier, Jesus told His disciples, "I am the way, the truth, and the life" (John 14:6). Evidently, the Spirit of truth longs to guide us into the Truth Himself—the person of Jesus Christ. That means God's desire for His children is that they be completely submerged, completely infused into Jesus, and the Holy Spirit is the One who does the submerging.

> ... for he shall not speak of himself; but whatsoever he shall hear, that shall he speak (John 16:13).

This reveals that the Holy Spirit did not come to represent or to put forth Himself; the purpose of His mission is to glorify another. And whatever is spoken to Him by the other two members of the holy trinity is then communicated to us. The Holy Spirit declares, reveals and glorifies Jesus. That is His ministry.

Some may think it sounds very spiritual to say, "I'm not all that interested in the Holy Spirit, speaking in tongues, miracles and stuff like that; I just want Jesus." But, friend, you cannot even begin to *know* Jesus or experience His fullness and richness apart from the infilling of the Holy Spirit in your life. The mighty

Spirit of God makes the ministry of Jesus real, active and present in the lives of those who open their hearts to Him. Apart from an ongoing, intimate relationship with the Holy Spirit, we as believers will never know the riches and the glory of God's plan and purpose for our lives or know the fullest measure of His ministry in the Church.

CHAPTER 4

GIFTS OF THE SPIRIT IN THE CHURCH TODAY

A spiritual phenomenon swept through America in the 1970s with the force of a blazing wildfire. It was a sovereign move of God that changed the landscape of Christianity. This movement was termed the Charismatic Movement, or Charismatic Renewal, based on the Greek word *charis,* which is translated as *spiritual gifts* in 1 Corinthians 12:1.

This chapter in Paul's first letter to the Corinthian church, as well as Chapter 14, outline the gifts, or supernatural manifestations, of the Holy Spirit. These demonstrations of divine power, revelation and utterance functioned through ordinary believers who had received the gift of the Holy Spirit and marked the miraculous nature of the early church.

It is a historical fact that these God-given phenomena were active in church history here and there throughout its more than 2,000 years of existence. But at some point after the third century, these spiritual gifts declined as the church became less a powerful tool of world evangelization and instead grew into a political and religious hierarchy more enamored with titles, position and secular power than in caring about the souls of men.

Nevertheless, there was a widespread resurgence of the New Testament experience of the baptism of the Holy Spirit, accompanied by spiritual gifts, or *charismata,* in the last half of the 20th century. Even though the body of Christ had become fragmented into multiple denominational groups, the walls of preference, pride and prejudice were not high enough to contain this flood tide of the fresh outpouring of God's Spirit.

This move of God breathed new life into a Church resembling an ailing patient on life support. Through the decades of the 20th century the Church had become increasingly liberal, compromising its theology and apathetic in its efforts to evangelize the world. But as a result of the Charismatic Movement, the Church began to arise from its spiritual slumber. The Church had become a sleeping giant, but the giant was beginning to wake up.

What made this movement so unique was not the fact that folks were being filled with the Holy Spirit and speaking in tongues, prophesying and operating in spiritual gifts or laying hands on sick folks and casting out devils like the believers in the Acts church. What made this move so strikingly different from past moves of God was the fact that these things were happening to people who were staunch members of denominations who preached against and discouraged these types of spiritual activities.

Spiritual gifts were alive and well and fully operative in the Full Gospel or Pentecostal denominations in the United States and around the world. But for believers from the mainline evangelical, non-Pentecostal churches to flow in these manifestations of the Holy Spirit was nothing short of astounding. Surely this was the imprint of the hand of God. Christians from every major denomination testified of a resurgence of intimacy with God, a new found joy in their Christian lives and a sense of boldness and power never before experienced. Many reported that after receiving this baptism of the Holy Spirit, their relationship with God took on a greater depth and meaning than ever before.

And yet, as widespread and influential as the Charismatic Movement was, it was not without its shortcomings and excesses. But that really should not surprise us. Church history reveals that nearly every significant outpouring of the Holy Spirit in the Church, including the original one in the first century church, was marked in two different ways. On one hand, these outpourings were accompanied by genuine, heaven-sent manifestations of the Holy Spirit. But on the other hand, there were questionable and even spurious spiritual occurrences. It shouldn't surprise us then that whenever God originates something holy, pure and beneficial in the Church, the devil will immediately work to devise a dark counterfeit. It's Satan's attempt to create an unholy, cheap imitation to deceive and mislead innocent seekers of God's genuine presence and blessing.

Be that as it may, even though some questionable practices may have taken place and some false doctrine taught by some misguided souls, droves of believers were experiencing a new Pentecost. The Holy Spirit was once again coming upon believers as He had in Acts, and believers were operating in spiritual gifts just like their counterparts in the first church.

Yet, amidst all the excitement and energy this refreshing new wind of the Holy Spirit breathed into the Church, many religious leaders opposed this new thing the Lord was doing in the historical churches. It took many leaders by surprise and upended the prevailing theology of many prominent church officials. How could this new movement be scriptural? This resurgence of Holy Spirit activity ran crosswise with commonly accepted beliefs, creeds and doctrines of what constituted "normal and orthodox" church activity and practice.

Most Christian churches subscribed to very definite, if narrow, ideas about the Holy Spirit. Of course they acknowledged the Holy Spirit as a divine personality, the third person of the triune godhead. But when it came to a present-day, supernatural ministry of the Spirit in the Church, religious eyebrows were raised and debates began to ignite across the Christian landscape. The Charismatic Movement bumped up against popularly accepted beliefs that most Christians had been taught all their lives. Unfortunately, too many people had simply acknowledged what they had been taught as being valid without really taking the time to rightly divide the Word and see what the scriptures *really* taught.

For example, when it came to the miraculous aspect of Christianity, such as the baptism in the Holy Spirit, speaking in tongues and divine healing being operative in the Church today, the standard response was, "That was just for the early Church" or "Those things passed away when the last Apostle died." In fact, variations on these same positions have circulated throughout the church world for centuries. Some have taught that the gifts of the Spirit were meant to be confirmatory or foundational in nature and in operation. In other words, some have purported that these gifts of the Holy Spirit were intended to be temporary in nature and only for the church in Acts.

> FOR AS LONG AS THE CHURCH IS PRESENT IN THE EARTH, IT WILL BE ENDOWED WITH THE HOLY SPIRIT AND HIS GIFTS.

Those who espouse this explanation point out that spiritual gifts were necessary to *start* the young church. Unfortunately they also believe that after the church was birthed in the mighty power and glory of the Holy Spirit, the accompanying spiritual phenomena was no longer required after the completion of the New Testament canon of scripture. There is only one problem with this logic: It isn't scriptural.

Nowhere in the Bible is it even remotely suggested that there will be a time in the Church Age when these supernatural manifestations will no longer operate among believers filled with the Holy Spirit. For as long as the Church is present in the earth, it will be endowed with the Holy Spirit and His gifts. However, having made this point, it is certainly true that there will be a time when this particular aspect of the Spirit's ministry will no longer be needed. The Word of God clearly reveals this to us in 1 Corinthians 13.

> Charity never faileth: but whether there be prophecies, they shall fail; whether there be tongues, they shall cease; whether there be knowledge, it shall vanish away. For we know in part, and we prophesy in part. But when that which is perfect is come, then that which is in part shall be done away (1 Corinthians 13:8-10).

This is the scripture used by many to support the claim that the supernatural ministry of the Holy Spirit as it relates to speaking in tongues, divine healing and other such manifestations have ceased functioning in the church today. Theologians have subscribed to this theory for years and have even given it a name: the Cessation Theory.

Yet, this scripture in 1 Corinthians 13 is the *only* scripture in all the Word of God that even deals with the aspect of the cessation of spiritual gifts in the Church. Think about it. One scripture in God's Word that points to a time when operations of God's Spirit will no longer be necessary in the Church and from *one* scripture men have built an entire doctrine. They insist that these divinely granted heaven-sent endowments of God's power—God's mind and His will to the Church—are no longer needed in the work of proclaiming the gospel. At best, that's using a flawed and faulty means of Bible interpretation, and at worst, it's dishonest and terribly misleading.

Consider the following verses of scripture:

> ... in the mouth of two or three witnesses
> every word may be established (Matthew
> 18:16).

> ... in the mouth of two or three witnesses
> shall every word be established (2
> Corinthians 13:1).

In these scriptures, both Jesus and the apostle Paul have given us a safe and reliable guide concerning proper Bible interpretation. In order to establish sound doctrine, it is necessary that the scripture supporting a particular teaching appear in the Bible more than one time. In fact, the truth being discussed must be found in at least two or three references in the Word of God in order to form a solid foundation for doctrine and practice. If we want to know the mind of God on any Bible subject, we can be sure it will appear in many places in scripture.

False doctrines and error come about when scriptures are isolated and presented as the whole truth on any given subject. And that is precisely what men have done with these verses in 1 Corinthians 13. Unfortunately, for the most part, the Church has accepted the ideas of men more so than the Word of a God who cannot lie. Let's examine these scriptures in detail and find out what they *really* teach.

> Charity [love] never faileth: but whether
> there be prophecies, they shall fail; whether
> there be tongues, they shall cease; whether
> there be knowledge, it shall vanish away.
> For we know in part, and we prophesy in
> part. But when that which is *perfect* is
> come, then that which is in part shall be
> done away. When I was a child, I spake as a
> child, I understood as a child, I thought as a

child: but when I became a man, I put away
childish things. For *now* we see through a
glass, darkly; but *then* face to face: *now* I
know in part; but *then* shall I know even as I
am known (1 Corinthians 13:8-12).

There it is—the sum total of instruction from God's Word
outlining the time when the gifts of the Spirit will no longer
be necessary in the Church. Let's take a closer look at what's
being said. Obviously, Paul teaches in these verses that there
will be a time when these spiritual gifts will one day pass away.
He alludes to this fact in verse 10 when he makes the statement,
"But when that which is *perfect* is come, then that which is in
part shall be done away."

However, by the inspiration of the Holy Spirit, Paul also
makes the point that the gifts will only cease to be necessary
when what he terms *perfection* arrives. Therefore, in order to
rightly determine when these manifestations will cease, we must
have a proper understanding of not only when this perfection
will come, but also what *perfection* here really means.

It's been commonly taught by some that the perfection
Paul discusses here refers to the time when the canon of New
Testament scripture would be completed, and therefore there
would be no further need of spiritual gifts to function in the
Church. Those who subscribe to this belief argue that the word
Paul uses for *perfect* in verse 10 is the Greek word *teleios,* which
means *perfect, mature or complete.* They reason that perfection
was achieved when the New Testament writings were completed.
But it takes a giant leap of logic to arrive at this conclusion. For
a number of reasons, Paul could not be referring to the finished
New Testament writings when he uses the word *perfect.* Let's
look at a few reasons why this is so.

Remember, we said earlier that proper Bible interpretation
demands that we cite two or more witnesses in scripture to
establish sound doctrine. Applying this rule, one of the best

ways to understand what Paul meant by the Greek word *teleios* would be to carefully examine every place he used the word in scripture. Then we can see how Paul normally used this word when he spoke, and thereby, we can understand exactly what he meant when he used this word.

Apart from this verse in 1 Corinthians 13, Paul used *teleios* seven other times in his writings:

> And be not conformed to this world: but be ye transformed by the renewing of your mind, that ye may prove what is that good, and acceptable, and *perfect [teleios]* will of God (Romans 12:2).

> Howbeit we speak wisdom among them that are *perfect* ... (1 Corinthians 2:6).

> Brethren, be not children in understanding: howbeit in malice be ye children, but in understanding be *men [teleios]* (1 Corinthians 14:20).

In the Bible I use in my personal study and preaching, there is a note at the bottom of the page of this scripture in 1 Corinthians 14 indicating the word *men* in this verse means "perfect or of a ripe age."[1]

> Till we all come in the unity of the faith, and of the knowledge of the Son of God, unto a *perfect* man ... (Ephesians 4:13).

> Let us therefore, as many as be *perfect,* be thus minded ... (Philippians 3:15).

> Whom we preach, warning every man, and teaching every man in all wisdom; that we may present every man *perfect* in Christ Jesus (Colossians 1:28).

> Epaphras, who is one of you, a servant
> of Christ, saluteth you, always laboring
> fervently for you in prayers, that ye may
> stand *perfect* and complete in all the will of
> God (Colossians 4:12).

Every one of these verses cited, with the exception of Romans 12:2, refers not to the completion of the New Testament writings, but rather with the spiritual maturity of the saints. When Paul uses the word *telios* he is talking about being made perfect or fully mature in Christ. If Paul uses the word *telios* in all these verses to describe the believers' spiritual development, why would he all of a sudden switch gears and decide to use the word *perfect* to refer to the completion of the New Testament? It simply doesn't make sense.

For one to teach that Paul is dealing with the finalizing of New Testament writings, 1 Corinthians 13:10 would be completely out of context given the things he discussed throughout the entire chapter. But there is ample evidence to support the fact that Paul was discussing the future spiritual perfection of believers that will occur at the resurrection of the dead. As Paul pointed out two chapters later in 1 Corinthians 15:

> Behold, I tell you a mystery: We shall not
> all sleep, but we shall all be changed—in a
> moment, in the twinkling of an eye, at the
> last trumpet. For the trumpet will sound,
> and the dead will be raised incorruptible, and
> we shall be changed. For this corruptible
> must put on incorruption, and this mortal
> *must* put on immortality (1 Corinthians
> 15:51-53 NKJV).

Paul describes here in absolute detail the completion—or perfection—of our salvation that will transpire when we receive our transformed, immortal bodies at the time of the catching away of the Church. As we've observed, Paul's consistent use of the word *teleios* in reference to the believers' spiritual maturity or completion makes it abundantly clear that the perfection he talks about in 1 Corinthians 13:10 is our final, ultimate perfection in heaven. There is absolutely no evidence to suggest that Paul had in mind the completion of New Testament canon of scripture in this verse.

The Williams New Testament records verse 10 in this manner: *"But when perfection comes, what is imperfect will be set aside." Young's Literal Translation* renders the phrase this way: "But when full understanding comes, these partial things will become useless."

It is clear from the context in verse 10 that the words *imperfect* and *these partial things* refer to the necessity and use of the gifts of the Holy Spirit now in this present Church age. In no way did Paul suggest that the Holy Spirit is imperfect or that His gifts are imperfect. But we must realize that these manifestations of the Holy Spirit only will be needed while we remain in these fallen, mortal, physical bodies on planet Earth.

The truth is, it is the *use* of these spiritual gifts that is imperfect. This is what Paul is talking about when He says, "... for we know in part, and we prophesy in part...." But then he goes on to say, "when perfection comes...," referring to the attainment of the fullness of our salvation at the time of the rapture of the Church. Of course, when we're gathered together with all the saints of God in heaven, we will no longer have need of the gifts of the Spirit. Why? Paul answers that question by explaining in verse 12, "... for then shall I know even as also I am known."

If you will take the time to carefully study the scriptures that refer to this catching away, or the rapture, of the Church, you will learn that believers at that moment will be changed in the twinkling of an eye from mortality to immortality. Our previously mortal, fallen state of existence will be completely done away with when perfection comes. Hallelujah!

Yet, again, it is the completion and the perfection of our salvation Paul was referring to in these verses, not the completion of the New Testament. To adopt this erroneous position is to read something into these verses that simply is not there.

Another reason that refutes this New Testament Completion theory is simply that Paul never mentioned this subject in any of his writings to the churches. Paul never even talked about a New Testament or a completed collection of scriptures in any of his epistles. We need to keep in mind that every book in the New Testament written by Paul was a letter to a particular church or written to believers in a particular region where he had established personal relationships during the course of his ministry.

Paul referred to these writings as *letters*, not as new books of scripture. Of course, we now recognize that they are indeed the infallible, inerrant and divinely inspired Word of God because it was through the inspiration of the Holy Spirit that Paul was able to write them in the first place. Look with me at the following verses to see how Paul referred to his writings:

> I wrote you before in an epistle [a letter]
> not to company with fornicators (I
> Corinthians 5:9).

> For though I made you sorry with a *letter,*
> I do not repent, though I did repent : for I
> perceive that the same *epistle* hath made
> you sorry, though it were for a season (2
> Corinthians 7:8).

> That I may not seem as if I would terrify
> you by *letters* For his *letters,* they
> say, are weighty and powerful; but his
> bodily presence is weak, and his speech
> contemptible. Let such a one think this, that

such as we are in word by letters when we
are absent, such will we be also in deed when
we are present (2 Corinthians 10:9-11).

And when this epistle (letter) is read among
you, cause that it be read also in the church
of the Laodiceans ; and that ye likewise read
the epistle from Laodicea (Colossians 4:16).

I charge you by the Lord, that this *epistle*
be read unto all the holy brethren
(1 Thessalonians 5:27).

There are many more such instances where Paul refers to his
writings as letters. So again, we simply have no scriptural basis
for taking Paul's statements in 1 Corinthians 13:8-12 to mean a
completion of the New Testament because Paul never mentioned
a New Testament in the letters he wrote to the young churches.

Finally, notice something Paul said in the first letter he wrote
to believers in Corinth:

So that ye come behind in no *gift*; waiting
for the coming of our Lord Jesus Christ (1
Corinthians 1:7).

This scripture is important to us for a number of reasons.
Remember, we are asking the question: *Were spiritual gifts
intended to cease after the early church?* In this verse Paul is
commending the Corinthian believers for receiving the gifts of
the Holy Spirit. He notes that they do not lack in any of the
Spirit's manifestations. He further observed that they should, in
fact, expect to continue in the operation of these *charismata*, or
gifts of the Spirit, until the return of the Lord Jesus.

In other words, Paul makes it very clear that the gifts of
the Spirit were not intended to cease at some arbitrary point
in church history. Instead, they will no longer be needed when

Jesus comes to receive His glorious Church to Himself. At that point we will know, even as we are known. We will no longer be "seeing through a mirror darkly." The material, physical and earth-bound limitations of the flesh will be no more. And there will no longer be a need for a spiritual equipping that was only necessary on earth while the Church labors in the Lord's vineyard, joyfully awaiting His return for us.

PAUL MAKES IT VERY CLEAR THAT THE GIFTS OF THE SPIRIT WERE NOT INTENDED TO CEASE AT SOME ARBITRARY POINT IN CHURCH HISTORY.

Given the scriptures we've reviewed here and the correct interpretation of them, it seems very clear that the argument that the nine gifts of the Holy Spirit are no longer needed in the Church today is simply not valid and cannot be substantiated by God's Word. I believe we've made a compelling case that these things are part and parcel of the gospel of Christ and that every Christian can lay claim to these wonderful manifestations of the Holy Spirit as part of his legal inheritance in Christ Jesus.

The baptism of the Holy Ghost with the accompanying evidence of speaking in other tongues is a New Testament experience available to every believer. One must go outside the parameters of Holy Scripture in order to defend an opposite viewpoint on this subject.

F.F. Bosworth, in his classic work *Christ the Healer,* offers the following observation:

> The Holy Spirit came to execute for us
> all the blessings purchased by Christ's
> redemption, and pledged by the seven
> redemptive names. He has never lost any
> of His interest in the work he came to
> do. If you wish to know how He wants to
> act today, read how He did act. The Book

of Acts shows us how He wants to act
throughout all the days, even unto the end
of the age.

It was the Holy Spirit Who worked all the
miracles of healing at the hands of Christ.
Jesus never undertook a miracle until, in
answer to His prayer, the Holy Spirit, the
Miracle Worker, came upon Him, and then,
in full reliance upon the Spirit, He cast out
devils and healed the sick. The miracles of
Christ were all done by the Spirit in advance
of His own dispensation, or before He had
entered officially into office. Why would
the Holy Spirit, Who healed the sick before
His dispensation began, do less after He
entered office? Did the Miracle Worker enter
office to do away with miracles during His
own dispensation?

Bosworth continues:

Is the teaching and the practice of the
Church in the matter of healing [and for
that matter all the gifts of the Holy Spirit]
in this Laodicean [or lukewarm] period of
her history a truer expression of the will of
God than the teaching and practice of the
Early Church while under the full sway of the
Spirit? Decidedly not! I hesitate not to say
that modern theology has robbed the Holy
Spirit of a part of His ministry.[2]

Challenging those who maintain the position that miracles
and divine healing have been done away with, Rev. Bosworth
makes the point that it would be ludicrous to believe that the
Holy Spirit would do less in this present and full dispensation of
the Holy Spirit's ministry than He did prior to it. He was poured

out upon the Church at Pentecost. We are presently living under the full expression of the office and ministry of the Holy Spirit, whereas in the Old Testament we read of Him at work here and there in the lives of a select class of individuals. Under the old covenant, He came upon certain individuals in power and enabled them to accomplish mighty exploits in the name of the Lord. But today—in this dispensation—we are experiencing the fulfillment of Joel's prophecy when he said that the Spirit of God would be poured out upon all flesh. The Holy Spirit has now taken up residence inside the hearts of believers and is now free to operate in His fullness through them.

And just as He manifested Himself through what we call the "gifts" of the Spirit in the first century church, so He does today. There was no arbitrary line drawn by the hand of God rendering the Holy Spirit's manifestations as no longer necessary in the Church. The fact is, these wonderful workings of the Holy Spirit have never been withdrawn and relegated to a previous time in church history—at least not as far as God is concerned. If spiritual gifts have ceased to function in the Church, the fault lies squarely upon our own faithlessness, our doubt and on a liberal, modernist approach to theology that strips the Word of its supernatural nature.

From time to time, we've read of accounts of daring jewel heists that took place by thieves who stole precious gems worth a fortune. Because these crooks were so cunning and crafty, they were able to successfully steal diamonds and other precious stones from their rightful owners. Many were never apprehended for their crimes because they were so adept at thievery.

Likewise, the devil is also a thief who comes to steal, to kill and to destroy. I believe that the most significant and costliest jewel theft in the history of the world pales in comparison to the theft of the manifestations of the Holy Spirit in the present-day Church. Satan, working through unwise men and misguided theologians, has caused much of the Church to be stripped of something much more valuable than precious stones. We've been robbed of the joy and the privilege of working in partnership with our Lord in the gifts of the Spirit to aid in preaching the gospel to the poor, to heal the brokenhearted, to bring freedom to captives and to liberate those who are battered and bruised in life.

We've allowed ourselves to be religiously brainwashed by scripturally illiterate theologians and teachers who've unwittingly been used as tools of the enemy to perpetrate false and misleading doctrines of devils upon the Church. We've allowed doctrines devised by mortal men created to fit a particular denominational mold that holds to an erroneous cessation theory to rob the Church of something God intended we should have. Let's face it. It's easier to teach that these things no longer operate in the Church than it is to study the Bible and exercise faith to be used in these spiritual manifestations. It really comes down to spiritual laziness and apathy.

It would not be an exaggeration to say that because of our lack of knowledge in these areas, and our ignorance of the Word of God on this subject, much of the Church world lives in total ignorance of spiritual understanding. In fact, we did the exact opposite of what Paul instructed when he said:

> Now concerning spiritual gifts, brethren, I would
> not have you ignorant (1 Corinthians 12:1).

As far as much of the modern Church is concerned, Paul may just as well have written the believers and said the following. "Dear believers: Please try to be as ignorant of the gifts of the Spirit as you can possibly be." If there is any one Bible subject the Church is more ignorant of than this particular area, I don't know what it could be. A vast segment of the body of Christ has pretty much bought into the lie that these things were intended only for the early church. On the other hand, the Pentecostal/

Full Gospel crowd is aware of spiritual gifts, but in many of their churches the operation of these gifts is nearly nonexistent.

You will notice that in the King James Version, the above verse has the word *gifts* in italics. That means this word was not found in the original manuscripts that formed the basis of our present-day Bible. It was added by the translators of the 1611 King James Authorized Version of the scriptures. The original rendering of this verse should read as follows:*"Now concerning spirituals, brethren, I would not have you ignorant."* Another way of understanding this verse is found by studying the original Greek phrasing of this scripture, which reads: "Now concerning things of, and pertaining to, the Holy Spirit, I would not have you ignorant."

Consider these additional translations of 1 Corinthians 12:1:

> Now about the spiritual gifts [the special endowments of supernatural energy], brethren, I do not want you to be misinformed (AMP).

> But about the things of the Spirit, my brothers, it is not right for you to be without teaching (BBE).

> Now, dear brothers and sisters, regarding your question about the special abilities the Spirit gives us. I don't want you to misunderstand this (NLT).

I believe Paul's insistence that the Church be grounded in the things of the Spirit was based on his desire that believers know what they've been freely given by God, so we can walk in a greater measure of the revelation of Jesus Christ. Without this extra dimension of God's Spirit in a believer's life, there's little real power to share the message of Jesus with the masses of the world. The Holy Spirit is the power who enables us to effectively share the message of salvation to the lost, bring healing to the sick and deliverance to those held in the grip of sin and bondage to the devil.

The world lies in the throes of a greater darkness and wave of evil and lawlessness than perhaps at any time in human history. How will the Church be able to penetrate the demonic forces, the sin and the depravity in our world today? By employing better public relations gimmicks? By doing more advertising? Attempting new church programs that originate in the minds of men? No, my friend, the Church only will be successful in her mandate of rescuing lost humanity when she rises up in faith and the power of the Holy Spirit to effectively duplicate the ministry of Jesus Christ. We must accomplish the same works He did by the same power Jesus flowed in—the power of the Holy Spirit.

> THE HOLY SPIRIT IS THE POWER WHO ENABLES US TO EFFECTIVELY SHARE THE MESSAGE OF SALVATION TO THE LOST, BRING HEALING TO THE SICK AND DELIVERANCE TO THOSE HELD IN THE GRIP OF SIN AND BONDAGE TO THE DEVIL.

We've tried everything else. We've tried promotional programs and have attempted nearly everything under the sun. Still, we've not had the worldwide impact the Church was designed to have. We've tried visitation programs, where people are visited in their homes and invited to come to church. In some cases those visited are presented with the plan of salvation and given an opportunity to receive Christ.

While these efforts at evangelism are certainly commendable, there is simply no substitute for God's program of sending forth believers ablaze with the power of the Holy Spirit, fully equipped with the ability of God. God sends believers to not only tell people about Jesus, but also to demonstrate a Living Christ.

You see, we're not called to merely recite the facts of Christ's resurrection to people who are lost, but we are to minister to people the same way Jesus did. According to Jesus' own words in Luke 4:18-19, He declared Himself to be anointed by the Holy Spirit to preach the gospel and bring healing to those who are sick. Now we have the ability through these heaven-sent spiritual gifts to not only preach, or proclaim the saving power of Christ, but also to provide God with a suitable habitation, a vessel through whom the Lord can touch the hurting.

I believe we've made a strong case for the continued operation of the gifts of the Holy Spirit in the Church today. The overwhelming evidence for this lies in what the scriptures have to say on the subject—not what some man or some denominations may believe about it. Nevertheless, people are strange creatures. Change for many people is difficult. We get comfortable in our own opinions and in what we hold to be true when it comes to deeply held religious beliefs.

Two things people are very opinionated about are politics and religion. Both topics represent strong personal convictions for most people. Yet, the question we must all face is whether or not we will be willing to humble ourselves and change when we are confronted with new light on a particular subject. We must decide if we have what it takes to adjust our opinions and attitudes when we're presented with factual evidence that proves our opinions and attitudes wrong.

What the scriptures teach concerning the gifts of the Spirit in the Church, and what men or even whole denominations may think about these things, may be vastly different. For centuries creeds and doctrines have been formulated and accepted as Bible truth based on what a group of men think about the Holy Spirit—as opposed to what rightly divided, properly interpreted scripture reveals about the Holy Spirit. As a result, huge numbers of earnest followers of Jesus Christ are being unwittingly deprived of something God intended to give them, something for which their hearts yearn.

Hosea 4:6 says, "My people are destroyed for lack of knowledge .... " And nowhere is this statement more apparent than in this area of the manifestation of the Holy Spirit. Yet, how responsible will the Lord hold those who teach against these things? After all, the Lord saw fit to devote two entire chapters (1 Corinthians 12 and 14), nearly the entire book of Acts and several other scriptures throughout the New Testament to reveal the guidelines and operations of these gifts in the church.

Yet even though we have the mind of God expressed thoroughly on this topic, it would be fair to say that most views and teachings concerning the Holy Spirit and His ministry contain only a portion of the whole truth. Each group, whether Methodist, Baptist, Presbyterian, Episcopalian, Pentecostal or others believe their particular view to be the only correct one. Each group uses— and at times misuses—scriptures to defend its positions and will strongly oppose those who see things differently.

But I strongly believe that if, in sincerity and humility, we will prayerfully study the entire body of truth on the subject of spiritual gifts and ask the Lord for illumination on these things, we will come away with the Lord's view—not our own. We need to ponder deeply these truths in God's Word until we become absolutely convinced of them. Then, and only then, will we rise up clothed with these wonderful gifts of the Holy Ghost given to help us make Christ fully known in our generation.

As we conclude this chapter, it would be good for us to have a historical understanding of the context in which these gifts were placed in the body of Christ in the first place. Then we would have a better understanding of why they were bestowed on the early believers and why they are still so desperately needed in our day.

Christianity had its origin when the Roman Empire was master of the world. Spiritually speaking, the Roman influence was corrupt, violent and rotten to the core. The glory of Greece was on the decline and, like Rome, was a very licentious and immoral culture. Aside from the land of Israel, the entire known world was caught up in idolatry and greatly influenced by demonic activity.

The religions of Rome, Greece and Egypt employed an ungodly mix of unclean and degrading practices. Demons were worshipped as gods, and as a result, a steady stream of false signs and wonders were performed by the priests of these religions. We must keep in mind that in the realm of the supernatural, there is a dark side. Satan is a spirit being, and he is crafty, cunning and skilled in the practice of deception and manipulation. He is capable of mimicking the hand of God to a certain degree in order to manifest counterfeit signs and wonders.

These religions, false as they were, had a powerful hold on the people who were under the sway of these hellish influences. Superstition was the order of the day. These demonic gods were regularly called upon to impart certain directive signs to people.

History reveals that before Julius Caesar crossed the Rubicon to enter Italy and fight against Pompei and eventually become ruler of the whole Roman Empire, his soothsayers, or practitioners of the black arts, would kill sacrificial birds and then read the signs within their dead bodies. In Egypt the goddess Isis was worshipped and through incantations her devotees called forth demons who performed cures to heal certain diseases.

Scattered over the known world at that time were shrines and temples erected for the purpose of worshipping false gods. Possibly the most notable among them was the Temple of the Goddess Diana at Ephesus, a city where Paul preached and God's power was released in a mighty way. Diana's followers believed that great benefits would come to them.

The god Apollo was worshipped at Delphi. A temple was built in his honor there, and over a crevice in the rocks, poisonous vapors would ascend upward. Worshippers of Apollo would become stupefied by the drug-like effects of the vapors. Demons would then enter the bodies of the people and cause them to dance hysterically and even prophesy. Sometimes in other shrines and temples, wine mixed with narcotic substances was used to produce this stupor. This is what Paul was referring to when he spoke of "... the cup of demons" (1 Corinthians 10:21).

It was into this dark morass of heathenism and rampant devil worship that Christianity burst onto the scene. The light of Christ came to pierce the dark shroud of deception and demonic control over the lives of the people. Against these false religions, superstitions and demonic powers, the power of Christ waged warfare and reigned supreme.

You can readily see that no religion based on weak and powerless doctrines of men could ever hope to make any serious inroads against such evil. No religion stripped of the genuine, supernatural power of the Living God could ever defeat and turn back the onslaught of those wicked, demon powers from hell. It takes power to overcome power, and the stronger power will always prevail.

Friend, God did not leave His Church powerless and at the mercy of the devil and his hosts. But He has, through the Holy Ghost, supplied all that the Church will ever need to confront and conquer them. God gave the Church power over the power of the enemy then, and He has never withdrawn that power. It is still available today through the means of the Word of God and the gifts of the Spirit that the early church had at its disposal.

How utterly foolish for anyone to think that in our day—when perversion, evil, violence, the threat of terrorism and the near total collapse of moral standards is all around us—that these forces can be overcome successfully with natural means. Make no mistake about it—the dominant forces at work in our world today are supernatural in nature. Only the supernatural power of God is sufficient to win against the warfare we face with Satan and his principalities and powers, and only the supernatural power of God is sufficient to bring men and women into the knowledge of the truth that will make them free. Only the glorious gospel of Christ has the power to impart salvation, and only the gospel preached with power can make a lasting impact in our world.

> **THE CHURCH TODAY IS AS MUCH IN NEED OF THE POWER OF THE LORD AND THE PRESENCE AND OPERATION OF THE HOLY SPIRIT AS THE FIRST CENTURY CHURCH WAS.**

Paul marched into the city of Ephesus—into a den of lions, the very stronghold of Satan himself—and boldly preached the gospel and cast out devils. This was a city wholly given over to evil influences, and yet, Paul confronted the enemy on his own turf and put him on the run. But Paul didn't accomplish this in his own power; it wasn't his oratorical skills that got the job done. Paul boldly preached and demonstrated the gospel with signs and wonders by the power of the Holy Spirit at work in him. When the people witnessed the genuine power of God, the Bible says:

> ... the name of the Lord Jesus was magnified and many that believed came, and confessed, and showed their deeds. Many of them also which used curious arts brought their books together, and burned them before all men: and they counted the price of them, and found it fifty thousand pieces of silver. So mightily grew the Word of God and prevailed (Acts 19:17-20).

The Church today is as much in need of the power of the Lord and the presence and operation of the Holy Spirit as the first century church was. In fact, because much of the Church in America has lacked this power, the influence the Church should have had in our society has increasingly waned in the last several years. This is not because the gospel has changed or because God has changed. Rather, the decline of church influence in our society has occurred because we only presented a portion of the gospel.

Only the gospel that agrees with a particular denomination's theology is preached in pulpits today. The supernatural aspect of the Christian faith is purposely eliminated by many who feel it unreasonable, unneeded and fanatical. But if we forsake this God-given miraculous aspect of God's Word, then it becomes of no more effect than any other religion vying for the hearts of men.

> Making the word of God of none effect
> through your tradition, which ye have
> delivered: and many such like things do ye
> (Mark 7:13).

If we subtract this supernatural aspect of Christianity, then all we have to offer people is a philosophy, a belief system with no supporting evidence to back it up. But people need more than philosophy. They need to hear about a Jesus who is still alive. They need to hear about a Jesus who still forgives the sinner, still heals the sick and still empowers believers with the Holy Ghost.

Will the real Church please stand up and dare to reclaim our great heritage of faith and power? Will the real Church please stand up and dare to throw off the shackles of men's traditions and theories and once more be that vessel God can use to save the lost and salvage suffering humanity?

CHAPTER 5

AMBASSADORS OF CHRIST

Now then we are ambassadors for Christ, as though God did beseech you by us: we pray you in Christ's stead, be ye reconciled to God (2 Corinthians 5:20).

The Bible uses a variety of colorful word pictures to describe the impact and reality Jesus makes in our lives as we begin our journey of faith with Him. These phrases are sprinkled throughout the New Testament to inform us that when Jesus assumed His lordship over our lives we didn't simply "turn over a new leaf" or "get religion." We didn't join a church or merely make a vow to God to forsake our old ways and try to do better. The truth is, when we submitted our life to Jesus, our entire spiritual nature was radically changed.

We literally became a brand-new creation in God's sight. The old, sinful, spiritual nature that dominated us and held us in bondage was eradicated, and we received a brand-new life, a brand-new nature. We received the life and nature of God Himself. We were transformed into a new creation in our inward being—a creation that never before existed.

In many ways the New Birth and its implications have never been fully comprehended. And yet, the Bible instructs us in plain language about things we should expect to see take place in our lives as a result of receiving the life and nature of God.

For instance, Jesus said that we are "the light of the world" (Matthew 5:14). Think for a moment about the function of light. Light pierces the darkness. Light overcomes the darkness. Light is more powerful than darkness. Imagine being in a room where every light is turned off and there is no window; it's so dark you cannot see your hand in front of your face. But if someone turned on a hallway light outside the room, suddenly even the smallest bit of light would shine underneath the door. Suddenly there would be illumination sufficient to see in the room what was previously hidden.

Christianity was intended to have the same effect on this world. As children of God, Jesus said that we are to be light in a dark and evil world. He said, "Let your light so shine before men, that they may see your good works, and glorify your Father which is in heaven." In other words, the new life inside us should be apparent to the people around us, especially to those in captivity to sin. They should be drawn to us. They should be attracted to us. In the same way that a moth is drawn to a flame, people should be drawn to us because of the light of Jesus Christ emanating from us. Jesus said this light would convince folks that we possess something they do not have, but desperately need.

Jesus also described Christians as the "the salt of the earth" (Matthew 5:13). Here is a word picture used to describe our purpose and function as members of Christ's body. Think about how salt is used. For hundreds of years it's been used to preserve meat and prevent it from spoiling. It acts against the natural process of decay by preventing bacteria from polluting the meat, keeping it pure and fresh.

We're living in a world that is rotten and putrefying because of the law of sin and death in the earth. The effects of sin and the fall of man are visible everywhere around us. God's original design has become so marred by sin and death that were it not for the restraining force of the Holy Spirit working in and through the Church, the rampant evil in our world would be totally intolerable. The Church—the salt of the earth—is positioned by God to prevent a total collapse of society. We are here to lift up a holy, righteous standard against the evil perpetrated by the enemy.

Our purpose is not to sit quietly in our churches huddled together like scared rabbits, safely tucked away inside the walls of our church buildings while Satan and his minions parade an endless stream of filth and perversion through our culture. That's exactly what the devil is hoping we will do. He's counting on the Church to remain mired in a haze of passivity and apathy, while the world around us marches onward to an eternity in hell. No, my friend, we have a voice, and it's the voice of righteousness. It's the voice we've been given to prepare the way of the Lord and to make the crooked places straight and the rough places smooth.

We are God's mouthpiece on the earth. Our task is to boldly speak the Word of the Lord and raise up a mighty banner for our God. We are not to simply look the other way and pretend evil doesn't exist. Rather, we should expose the evil deeds of darkness and bring the savor of the knowledge of God into the public arena. How? We must do so not simply with lip service, but rather by displaying a holy walk with God.

God is not interested in our displaying a false, "holier than thou" attitude; Jesus never did that. He loved the sinners He ministered to, and He demonstrated genuine concern for their souls. People recognized Jesus' love and compassion; they *felt* it. Yet, Jesus never compromised His righteousness while endeavoring to reach lost people with the Good News.

Another description given to believers is found in John 15:5, where Jesus said, "I am the vine, ye are the branches." He is the vine, or the trunk, of the tree. How descriptive this phrase is. Naturally speaking, the branches of a tree or plant derive their life from the sap that flows upward from the roots, bringing nourishment and energy to the entire organism. But it's important here to understand that the branches of the vine are where fruit production takes place. Jesus said if we remain vitally united with Him, we can expect to produce much fruit.

What kind of fruit? Jesus fruit. God is expecting us to display His life and His goodness. It's Jesus' life being ministered to people, but His life flows through us. What a privilege! As laborers together with the Lord, we must understand that not only do we desperately need the Lord every moment in our lives, but also in a very real sense, God needs us.

Redemption is the work of God. He's the only One who can save a soul, heal a body, deliver the oppressed and set the captives free. But He is relying upon us, His branches, to dispatch the report of the Lord, the message of truth that makes men free. That is our job.

That brings us to the next descriptive term illustrating our union with God. Paul writes in 1 Corinthians 12:27, "Now ye are the body of Christ, and members in particular." Our bodies are the body of Jesus Christ; we are bone of His bone, and flesh of His flesh (Ephesians 5:30). We are not "old sinners saved by grace," but rather, we are the embodiment of Christ on the earth. Among other things, a body serves as a vehicle through which personality, thought and action are expressed.

Man is threefold in composition, comprising spirit, soul and body (1 Thessalonians 5:23). So, in actuality, your body is not the truest expression of who you really are. Your body is simply the house *you* live in while residing on planet earth. Your body is a clothing of flesh for your spirit person within you who is the real you.

The body provides a means for the outward expression of our inner being, our spirit man. The spirit is ceaseless and eternal. The body will one day die and decay. Your spirit, or as Peter calls it, "the hidden *man* of the *heart*" (1 Peter 3:4), is the part of your being that provides and expresses personality, creativity and life. Your body responds to, and acts in accordance with, the impulses given it by your spirit and soul, which is the part of you having to do with the mind, the will and the emotions.

In the same way, Christ is the Head of the Church and we are the body. As His body we are to enact the will of Christ, the Head. We are to proclaim the Good News to folks, but it's the Holy Spirit who convinces the lost of their need of salvation. We lay hands on the sick, but it's the power of the risen Lord of glory who heals their bodies. We embrace the hurting and weep with those who weep, but it's the compassion of Christ that ministers to their broken hearts.

You see, God has no mouth with which to announce the Year of Jubilee, the year of the free favor of God extended to mankind, except it comes through our mouths. He has no hands to lay upon the sick and afflicted except it be our hands on them. He has no arms to comfort the grieving and the downcast, except ours. We *are* the body of Christ.

As believers we are Christ's ambassadors. We are those who have been fully deputized and authorized by the Master Himself to represent Him to the people of this world. We have been designated as His envoys, His messengers anointed by the Spirit of God to conduct kingdom business in His name.

Consider for a moment the responsibilities of an ambassador. The United States government dispatches ambassadors to foreign nations to represent the interests, the policies and the will of the government of the United States of America. The ambassador is not at liberty to express his or her personal convictions, at least not when conducting official U.S. business. The ambassador is only authorized to carry out the will of the government.

For all intents and purposes, an ambassador is the representative voice of the United States while residing in the nation where he or she serves. The ambassador is only authorized to speak and to act on behalf of the United States. When the ambassador faithfully expresses the will and convictions of the nation, then the U.S. government will support the ambassador, stand with the ambassador and back up his or her words.

As Christ's ambassadors, it's important we fully understand the One we represent. It's necessary that we know His interests, His desires and how He wishes to be represented. What is the message to mankind He wants us to speak on His behalf? After all, we do not represent ourselves. Neither are we called to represent a denomination. We are Christ's messengers. What is our message? The answer is simple: The same message Jesus proclaimed.

Paul said something worth noting about serving the interests of Christ in a letter he wrote to the Philippian Church.

> But I trust in the Lord Jesus to send
> Timotheus shortly unto you, that I also
> may be of good comfort, when I know your
> state. For I have no man likeminded, who
> will naturally care for your state. For all seek
> their own, not the things which are Jesus
> Christ's (Philippians 2:19-21).

Paul wanted to visit these believers himself in order to see how they were doing in their walk with God, but he couldn't. He was in prison. So he sent them a substitute. He chose someone who loved and cared for the people as much as he did. Paul thought about all the people he could send on this mission, and the only one he could trust to send was Timothy. Later on we read that a young man by the name of Epaphroditus also was sent by Paul to the Philippian believers.

Of all the men who traveled with Paul, ministered alongside him and helped him, only Timothy and Epaphroditus could be trusted to be sent to the Church at Philippi. Why? The other ministers Paul worked with were unreliable and untrustworthy. They didn't care about the plight of the church at Philippi; they were interested only in their own affairs. They were selfish and self-centered. They were focused on what pleased them. Sadly, they were like a lot of Christians today who are caught up in their own interests and pursuits, totally blind to the hurts and needs of others.

The New Living Bible translates verse 21 this way:

All the others care only for themselves and
not what matters to Christ.

Are there things that matter to Jesus that should matter to us? Absolutely. Are there things that concern Jesus in our world today that should concern us, His Church, His ambassadors? Unequivocally, yes. Does Jesus have any vital interests that we should share in as His body? Yes, indeed.

The Word is very clear that it is not God's will that any should perish or die in their sins, but instead, His will is that all would come to repentance. He desires that all men—everywhere—would experience a change of heart and turn their lives over to Him and receive the gift of eternal life, the life all mankind was created by God to live.

Jesus did not die on a cross and shed His precious blood in private where no one could see Him. Instead, He was stripped naked, beaten and made to suffer humiliation before crowds of people assembled in Jerusalem to celebrate the Feast of Passover. Jesus offered Himself as the supreme sacrifice for the sins of the world in full view of both His enemies and His followers.

The substitutionary sacrifice of Christ on that cruel Roman cross, where Jesus hanged like a common criminal of the day, was the greatest act of love the world has ever witnessed. It defied every notion of logic, reason and justice. Here was the very Son of God Himself, the Word made flesh, suffering the death of the lowest criminal element in all the Roman Empire. Here was the just suffering for the unjust, the righteous giving His life for the unrighteous. He who knew no sin being made sin for us on the cross. The unconditional love of God personified in the person of Jesus Christ.

As Christ's ambassadors, those chosen of God to be His envoys in the world, we must realize that the message of Christ's love for fallen humanity that we've been commissioned to deliver must be delivered not only in power, but also in love.

THE SUBSTITUTIONARY SACRIFICE OF CHRIST ON THAT CRUEL ROMAN CROSS, WHERE JESUS HANGED LIKE A COMMON CRIMINAL OF THE DAY, WAS THE GREATEST ACT OF LOVE THE WORLD HAS EVER WITNESSED.

Jesus said the world will recognize that we are His disciples when we have love one toward another (John 13:35) —when we demonstrate God's love to people. The phrase *love one another* appears some 14 times in the New Testament. Jesus used it five times in two consecutive chapters in the Gospel of John.

This unconditional love of God is not like natural, human love in that it expects nothing in return from the person to whom it is extended. There are no strings attached to it. It believes the best of people. It's not critical or judgmental toward others. This kind of love is willing to overlook the faults and imperfections of others. It gives the benefit of the doubt to folks who may be doing things wrong. Isn't this the way we want others to be toward us?

You may be thinking, *I would like to be able to relate to other people with the love of God. It sounds great, but I just cannot do it. There's no way I can be that way all the time. It's impossible. I try to be nice. I try to be tolerant with other people's shortcomings. But when it comes to loving people unconditionally, I just don't see how I can do it.* But friend, if it were simply a matter of us trying to muster up the willpower and the internal fortitude to love people in this way, we'd be defeated before we ever started.

The good news is that we don't have to try to walk in this wonderful, supernatural, God kind of love; it's already in us. What we need to do is learn how to yield to it, give place to it, and allow it to govern our life and conduct.

> The redeemed of the Lord are not only saved unto everlasting life; they are the children of God. When we say we are the children of God and that God is our Father we are not merely employing terms of inspiration or endearment; we are not making sentimental nor even devout reference to the One Who has in marvelous condescension taken up towards us an attitude of benevolence and loving-kindness. When we say that God is our Father and that we are His children, we are using terms of absolute relationship.
>
> We are not merely accepted of God: we are *begotten* of God. Our relationship to God is not one of divine courtesy but divine life. We are born of God. Our divine parentage is as real as, but infinitely more enduring than our human parentage. As children of God we are partakers now of His mighty, miraculous super-nature. Beloved, *now* are we the sons of God, partakers of His divine nature (2 Peter 1:4; 1 John 3:2). And God has made full provision for manifestation of that super-nature in His children in the gifts of the Holy Spirit." [1]

If the New Birth means we have been born anew—born from above—then it follows that in the act of re-creation we assumed the heavenly characteristics and abilities of the heavenly Father who caused us to be born anew. In the same way that the natural, physical and genetic characteristics of human parents are passed on to children in physical birth, so God's very own DNA is imparted to us when we receive His everlasting life.

In the act of regeneration, the Lord Jesus has stamped upon His begotten ones the imprint of His character and His life. In the baptism of the Holy Spirit, we are likewise clothed with the same power for ministry service that clothed Jesus Himself. As His ambassadors we need a full measure of both facets of the Holy Spirit's work in our lives in order to faithfully and accurately represent Jesus before people. We need the fruit of the Spirit to reflect the character of Christ, but we also need the gifts—or manifestations of the Spirit—to reflect the power of Christ. It's not one or the other; both facets of the work of the Holy Spirit are to be seen in the lives of Christians. Otherwise, how could we, the Church, ever hope to fulfill scriptures such as these:

> He that saith he abideth in him (Christ)
> ought himself also so to walk, even as he
> walked (1 John 2:6).

> Herein is our love made perfect, that we
> may have boldness in the day of judgment;
> because as he is, so are we in this world (1
> John 4:17).

Both aspects of this dual working of the Holy Spirit in the life of the believer are necessary if we are to fulfill God's plan for the Church to be just like Jesus. We've already dealt at some length with the aspect of the Spirit's anointing upon our lives, equipping and enabling us to do the same works in our day that Jesus did in His. But what about this other work of the Spirit as it relates to reproducing the character of Christ in us, in what the Bible calls the fruit of the Spirit?

> But the fruit of the Spirit is love, joy, peace, long suffering, gentleness, goodness, faith, meekness, temperance: against such there is no law. If we live in the Spirit, let us also walk in the Spirit (Galatians 5:22-23,25).

Why are these wonderful graces or virtues termed *fruit?* For the same reason that certain trees produce tasty, delicious red things with a stem and a core called apples. Apples are what grow on an apple tree. If the tree is healthy, and planted in good, fertile soil, and receives a sufficient amount of sunshine and water, it will produce the fruit known as apples.

The branches of the apple tree do not exert a great deal of effort and energy trying to grow apples. Neither must the apple trees devise new methods in order to inspire apples to grow. In fact, the branches really don't have to worry at all about whether or not there will be an apple crop. All that is necessary for normal apple production to occur is simply that the branches stay attached to the trunk of the tree. That is the key to successful production of delicious, juicy red, yellow or green apples year after year. If the branch stays fixed to the tree, apples will be the result.

Why? Because apples are the produce of the tree. And although apples grow on branches, the branches themselves are not solely responsible for apple production. You see, even though that is where the apples appear, the branches do not independently produce fruit all by themselves. Apples bud and blossom on the branch and turn into luscious fruit there, but apples don't begin there. Apples begin their life somewhere else—in the trunk of the tree, from the roots up.

In the trunk of the tree flows a substance called sap, which is the life-giving energy of the tree. Sap is liquid life that travels from the roots upward throughout the tree's trunk and then is distributed into the limbs and branches of the tree. The tree is alive and full of healthy, green leaves and fruit because of the sap flowing through it.

It isn't a matter of one part of the tree being more important than the other. Both are vitally needed if apples are going to grow on the tree. There must be the nutrient-rich, life-sustaining energy of the sap coursing its way through the entire tree, otherwise it could not produce and sustain life. On the other hand, there must also be a production center where apples grow and develop and become the tasty fruit that is the very reason for the tree's existence. Apples show off the life that is inside the tree; apples are *proof* of the life within the tree. Apples can be seen and experienced. Sap cannot—it's deep within the tree, invisible to the naked eye.

Similarly, then, we must bear fruit that begins deep within us at our Source. We must show off the life inside us and give proof of our relationship and association with the Holy One Who made us. If the Church is to be Christ's ambassador, then we not only represent Him in the power of the Holy Spirit, but we also must walk in the character of Christ through the power of the Holy Spirit.

> ... darkness shall cover the earth, and gross
> darkness the people (Isaiah 60:2).

The curse of sin has marred God's original design for his man. Instead of enjoying the glorious liberty and freedom of fellowship with God and experiencing His peace, people are mired in sin, confusion, selfishness and jealousy. The way of this world is every man for himself. People live this way because they don't know any better. They act out of their inner nature, which is one of death. Their unregenerate spirits and sinful carnal nature dictate to them every day the impulses that make them do the things they do. They are selfish because they are dominated by a selfish nature. Sinners commit sin because that is their nature.

But, friend, the world is starved for love—real love. God created man to receive and to live in His love. The deepest yearning of every human being is to be loved and to feel that someone cares about them. Every person alive possesses an inner urge to feel that they are somehow needed, valuable and important. This yearning so common to man can only be fulfilled by God's all-consuming love.

And that is where the Church comes in. This God kind of love must be demonstrated and seen if lost people are ever to have the opportunity of connecting with it. You and I, as envoys of heaven, as Christ's personal representatives, are called to show this love to the masses of selfish, unsaved people who have never heard the good news. We have been sent by God to display His goodness and His love. The world will never see God's love until believers learn to walk in the fullness of this most powerful force in the universe.

You are the open door through whom others can experience the unconditional love of God. Love is the wellspring from which all the fruit or characteristics of the Holy Spirit emanate. These nine fruit of the Spirit listed in Galatians 5 are the exact opposite of the works of the flesh dominating the life of the unregenerate or natural man.

Satan's nature is selfish and reproduces itself in the lives of his children. The world is full of selfish, unloving, greedy and downright hateful people who act just like their father the devil. But when we, the Church, make the quality decision to give place to the love of God shed abroad in our hearts by the Holy Spirit, then we will act like our Father. As we learn to live out of our hearts, and not from our fleshly nature, we will shine forth as bright lights in a dark world. When we yield to the promptings of the Holy Spirit within us, people around us will see the love of God in action. We as believers have the privilege of being the Lord's living, breathing billboards displaying the true nature of God.

Notice with me a compelling scripture in the Book of Titus, where Paul wrote to a young minister, one of his sons in the faith. The letter to Titus is similar to the two letters he wrote to Timothy. Paul shared practical advice with these young ministers that, if followed, would ensure success in their ministries.

A seasoned veteran of the faith and a man experienced at winning souls for Jesus, Paul knew that for the Church to fulfill its primary task of world evangelism it would be imperative for believers to walk in both dimensions of the Holy Spirit: the gifts of the Spirit for service and the fruit of the Spirit for character. Knowing this, he wrote the following to Titus:

> ...not purloining [stealing], but showing all good fidelity; that they (servants of Christ) may adorn the doctrine of God our Savior in all things (Titus 2:10).

Paul points out here, as well as other places in Titus, and in First and Second Timothy, that Christians are to "adorn the doctrine of God" or to adorn the gospel. The word *adorn* means *to decorate, to beautify, to enhance.* When you adorn something, you make it attractive and appealing. From this scripture, you can readily see that God's Word instructs that we are to make the gospel attractive to people. The gospel was designed to serve as a magnet to draw people to Christ as we demonstrate righteous behavior in the midst of a crooked and perverse generation.

As we've noted before, the world is accustomed to lying, selfishness, broken promises, and strife and discord. Many people we pass on the street, in the malls and at work are caught up in laziness, greed and irresponsibility. But the Church has both the privilege and the responsibility to manifest a whole new way of living—God's way of being. The goodness of God will attract the attention of people who don't have a personal relationship with Him. When we live our lives yielded to the Holy Spirit, the world will want what we have.

Our outward conduct—lives filled with the joy of the Lord and victory over sin, sickness and the works of the devil—stands in stark contrast to the misery and defeat of those without Christ. I'm convinced one of our greatest witnessing tools is the ability to "put on the new man" (Ephesians 4:24)—to "put on Christ"—and let the results of the New Birth show up on the outside.

> **WHEN WE LIVE OUR LIVES YIELDED TO THE HOLY SPIRIT, THE WORLD WILL WANT WHAT WE HAVE.**

Evidently, this was an extremely important concept to the apostle Paul as well. If you read through his letters to the churches, very often he deals with the subject of godly conduct. So, as ambassadors of the Lord Jesus Christ, will the real Church please stand up, full of faith, full of power and walking in godly character?

When we choose to allow the Holy Spirit to both empower us and conform us to the image of Christ in godly character, we will present an irresistible invitation to all men "to be saved and to come to the knowledge of the truth" (1 Timothy 2:3-4).

CHAPTER 6

THE GREATEST OF THESE IS LOVE

> A new commandment I give unto you, That
> ye love one another; as I have loved you,
> that ye also love one another. By this shall
> all men know that ye are my disciples, if ye
> have love one to another (John 13:34-35).

Jesus told His disciples the standard by which the world would
know we are His disciples. It won't be by how many times
a week we go to church, not by how much of the Bible we can
quote or how much faith we possess. It won't be by how loudly we
praise God or how many miracles we perform. All these things
are great, but Jesus said the world will know that we are His
disciples by our love.

Unconditional love is not critical or judgmental toward
others. This kind of love believes the best of people and is willing
to overlook peoples' faults and extend the benefit of the doubt to

them. Love recognizes that none of us is a completely finished product yet. God is continually working in our lives, perfecting that which concerns us.

Before we ever acknowledged the Lord and opened our hearts to Him, God was pursuing us. When we were enemies of God and alienated from Him, our unbelieving minds blinded by the deception of Satan, God was searching us out and doing His best to woo us to His heart of love.

All people everywhere are at varying degrees of both spiritual and mental maturity. Knowing this, it is important that we be willing to offer grace to people in the same way Jesus offered it to us. God is endeavoring to make Himself known to men and women the world over. He's dealing with people's hearts everywhere. So if someone makes a mistake and commits sin, we have no right to condemn, look down upon or treat them like a second-class citizen. Why? Because the love of God has been imparted to us. We are not to hold sinners in self-righteous contempt. Instead, we are to pray for them and have mercy on them.

> It is of the Lord's mercies that we are not consumed, because His compassions fail not. They are new every morning; great is Thy faithfulness (Lamentations 3:22-23).

After thinking about the wrong choices and mistakes you made in your own life, aren't you thankful the Lord forgave you and restored you with His mercy? The fact is, we've all sinned and come short of the glory of God. Of course we don't excuse sin and wrongdoing; we don't simply brush it off, saying, "Oh well, everybody misses it from time to time." But, at the same time, we must be careful not to assume the role of judge, jury and executioner when we see others caught in the throes of sin.

The Bible says God delights in mercy (Micah 7:8). Shouldn't we be the same way? If we observe a person mock and ridicule the things of God, even that does not exempt us from walking in love toward that person and treating them with dignity and respect.

It's very easy to love someone as long as they think like you, dress like you and believe the same way as you. Anyone can display love toward a person like that because we agree on everything. Yet Jesus did not say, "Love one another if you agree on everything and see eye to eye on every issue." The kind of love Jesus wants us to display is one that loves even a person who is completely different than we are.

> If you love only those who love you, what reward is there for that? Even corrupt tax collectors do that much (Matthew 5:45 NLT).

If we choose to love only those who are exactly like us, then we are putting ourselves on the same level as some of the greediest and most corrupt people who ever lived. But the Church has been called to exemplify a much higher and greater kind of love in the world. The essence of what Jesus was teaching here is that what a person believes or what kind of person they are should have no bearing on whether or not we choose to love them.

God's love doesn't care if a sinner is totally opposed to everything a believer holds to be sacred and precious; He still calls upon us to show love to them. There is already enough hatred and animosity in the world. In fact, if we Christians would stop being so critical and judgmental toward others who don't see things quite the same way as we do, and instead show God's love, acceptance and forgiveness, we would make a tremendous impact in this world for God. I believe we would experience the greatest spiritual awakening the world has ever witnessed if believers would simply humble themselves and show love to one another.

Even if others do things that are wrong or are living in sin, it's not our job to straighten them out. God never deputized us into His "sin patrol" to point out the faults of others. He never assigned Christians the responsibility of waiting and watching for people to get out of line so we can execute God's judgment on them and piously announce to them that they're on their way to hell. That's simply not our job. The Holy Spirit is the only One who has been sent from the Father to convince or convict the world of sin.

Our task is simply to be filled with God's love and compassion and take the good news to those we meet. The good news is not that people are going to hell. The good news is that Jesus has *already* paid an awesome price to make it possible for people to escape the wrath to come. The blood of Jesus has been shed for the remission of every person's sins. Now, we the Church, are to proclaim to the world liberty from sin, sickness and bondage. That's good news!

We are to share the message that God is not counting up and holding against men their sins. Instead, He has cancelled them out. Our message should be: God loves you, and He will receive you just the way you are. But when He does receive us, He loves us too much to allow us to remain the way we are. He binds up every wound. He removes the spiritual and emotional scars sin has brought to bear upon us. He heals our broken hearts. He lifts us up out of the miry clay of despair and gives us hope. Our God is a Redeemer!

This is our assignment. This is our message to the world, and it's the only message we've been authorized to preach. It is the goodness of God that leads men to repentance—not beating people up with the "truth," or pointing out all their misdeeds. Rather, it is the love and mercy of God flowing out of us that will change people's hearts.

When we focus on a loving, heavenly Father who loves unconditionally and chooses not to condemn us and hold sins over our heads as a continual reminder of our past failures, people will run after a God like that. That's the way God really is. And He has never changed. It is men who have incorrectly portrayed Him as a vengeful, vindictive God of wrath, waiting to inflict sore punishment upon people the moment they commit sin. But, the truth is, if people really knew what God was like, they would gladly receive His gift of love and mercy.

> For God sent not his Son into the world
> to condemn the world; but that the world
> through him might be saved (John 3:17).

I suppose the verse preceding this one is the most familiar and well-known scripture in all the Bible: "For God so loved the world, that He gave his only begotten Son, that whosoever believeth in him should not perish, but have everlasting life." This was the first scripture I ever memorized as a young boy in the Methodist church. Believers everywhere know this verse about God's great love for mankind, demonstrated by sending Jesus to ransom and rescue fallen man. But how much better would it have been if our church leaders had been equally determined to expound the truth of verse 17 as they have been to preach verse 16?

God sent His Son to save the sinner, not to condemn the sinner. God sent Jesus to earth glad, not mad. If Jesus, being perfect, blameless and without sin, chose not to condemn and pass judgment on sinners, then how can we as imperfect individuals possibly justify critical, judgmental attitudes toward them?

You cannot find one place in the four Gospels where Jesus condemned the sinner, but there are many instances where He roundly condemned the hypocrisy of the pious, self-righteous Pharisees and other misguided religious leaders. But when it came to those living in adultery, or those who lied and cheated others, Jesus looked beyond their outward transgressions. He looked through the eyes of compassion and saw people desperately searching for true peace and happiness.

For instance, in Chapter 4 of the Gospel of John, Jesus had an encounter with a Samaritan woman who was drawing water from a well. In the first place, for a Jewish man to have a private conversation with a woman in Samaria was unthinkable. It violated the cultural norms of the day involving interaction between Jews and Samaritans. But Jesus refused to allow the racial prejudice of the day to prevent Him from ministering God's love to a woman in need.

This woman had been married five times, and the man she was living with at the present time was not her husband. They were simply co-habiting together apart from the covenant of marriage. It would be easy to understand that a woman who suffered five failed marriages would in all likelihood have given up on the idea of marriage. Living with a man outside of marriage seemed to be for her a more reasonable alternative.

Imagine the gossip she must have endured from the other women in the village. No doubt, she was an outcast in the community. People looked down their noses at her. She was a hard-core sinner in their view.

Yet, notice what Jesus did and what he did not do. He did not condemn her, and He did not look down on her. He didn't say, "You evil, wicked sinner. Don't get too close to me and my disciples. We don't want to be contaminated by your vile sin." Instead, He simply loved her and told her about God. He looked beyond her sin and saw someone who needed to receive love and restoration from God. And she turned out to be the first person Jesus revealed Himself to as Messiah.

Jesus chose a woman living in sin over His disciples, over John the Baptist and over the religious leaders of the day to be the first to disclose who He was. What was the result of Jesus sharing God with this woman and restoring dignity to a woman who had such a bad reputation among the people?

> And many of the Samaritans of that city
> believed on Him for the saying of the
> woman, which testified, He told me all I
> ever did (John 4:39).

This woman's testimony about Jesus and the impact He had on her life, coupled with the fact that He knew by the Holy Spirit's revelation about her troubled life, resulted in a great number of people acknowledging Jesus as their Savior. The people who previously despised and shunned this woman had begun thanking her for sharing the good news about a God who forgives and restores.

Think how many glorious opportunities we've missed out on by avoiding people we thought were a bit too unsavory for us to be around. We've missed opportunities for effective evangelism, and we've missed the blessing of being God's channel through whom He could have poured out His love and forgiveness.

I remember an incident that occurred several years ago when my father served as a deacon in his church. One Sunday morning my father was greeting folks at the door as they made their way inside the church. The pastor happened to be standing nearby talking with someone, when a couple of young guys entered. This was during the early 1970s when many young men wore their hair long and dressed in blue jeans and T-shirts. These two young men sported longer-than-usual hair, and they weren't wearing suits and ties like most of the men in the church. Their clothing was clean, but certainly not dressy.

My dad greeted them and told them how glad he was that they had chosen to visit the church and be a part of the worship service. But when the pastor spotted the young men, he walked over to them and quickly informed them that they could not come inside "the house of God" looking the way they did. He told them that if they were willing to cut their hair short and wear "nicer" clothes, they would be welcome to come back to the church.

Obviously this pastor did not realize that because of his prejudice about the men's hair length and dress habits, he totally misrepresented the nature of God to them. Inadvertently, he communicated to them the message that a person must be nice, neat and well-groomed before God will welcome them in His house. His words and attitude toward these young men conveyed the idea that people who do not conform to socially accepted norms of dress and grooming will not be received by God. How tragic!

Those young men were searching—searching for truth, searching for answers, searching for God. Something told them they might find help and relief for the emptiness in their hearts in that church. So they went there hoping to find help. Maybe they were not even sure what they might encounter there. But the message they received loud and clear from the pastor was: "We don't want your kind here. How dare you defile the house of God, coming here dressed the way you are. We only want clean-cut, well-dressed folks. You two don't qualify to be here. God only loves 'nice' people."

What a missed opportunity. How tragic that this pastor allowed his own preconceived notions and personal preferences to blind him from being used by God to speak into the lives of these young men about the love, mercy, and acceptance of God. What a tragedy that he blew his chance to be the one God could use to share His love with these boys. What a golden opportunity to tell about a Jesus who loved these young men so much that He was willing to assume their guilt and sins and give them the gift of eternal life.

WE NEED TO LEARN TO WALK IN AS MUCH GRACE AS WE DO IN TRUTH; CERTAINLY JESUS WAS FULL OF BOTH.

The Bible says that when Jesus came to this sin-defiled, cursed earth, He did so "full of grace and truth" (John 1:14). Notice it didn't say that Jesus came simply with truth; the scripture said grace *and* truth. We need to learn to walk in as much grace as we do in truth; certainly Jesus was full of both.

So many believers are caught up in the letter of the law. They know all the scriptures that deal with judgment and condemnation, but they fail to appreciate all the scriptures that point out God's love, mercy and forgiveness. It's very easy to lift certain isolated scriptures out of the Bible and build doctrines around them. But if you carefully study the life of Jesus, you will see that the overriding quality of His life was His amazing love for people.

He displayed a tremendous compassion for people everywhere He went, especially to those stained by sin. In John 8 we read how the Pharisees brought to Jesus a woman caught in the act of adultery. These religious leaders reminded Jesus that according to the Law of Moses the woman deserved to be stoned to death. Believing they had trapped Jesus based on the demands of the law and leaving no escape for the woman, Jesus did something very strange. He stooped down and began writing in the dust of the ground with His finger. Then rising back up, He said to the angry mob that couldn't wait to put her death, "He among you that has never sinned, cast the first stone." One by one they all dropped their stones in shame and began to walk away, beginning with the oldest man down to the youngest.

Jesus turned to the woman and asked her, "Woman, where are your accusers? Isn't there anyone left to accuse you?"

She answered Him, "No man, Lord."

Jesus replied, "Neither do I condemn you; but go, and sin no more." It is clear from this account in Jesus' ministry that God does not in any way condone sin. He does not approve of men and women living together outside of marriage. The Bible calls this fornication, and it's wrong according to the law of God. But Jesus did not condemn her; He gave her another chance. He forgave her, restored her and cautioned her not to sin this way any more.

He gave her back a dignity and a worth she had lost a long

time ago. He let her know that God is in the restoration business. In fact, Jesus was the last great hope she would ever have of living a fulfilling and honorable life. Everybody else in her community had her pegged as a loser, someone to avoid and slander.

Friend, when we interact with people, we should not in any way look down on them or write them off as hopelessly lost. We should not condemn anyone. God is big enough to salvage anyone's life and give them a brand-new start.

This principle is illustrated further in Luke 19 as Jesus and His disciples passed through Jericho. As they walked along, Jesus spotted a man named Zacchaeus who was sitting in a tree to get a better look at Jesus as He passed by.

Zacchaeus was a chief tax collector in Jericho, and he was very rich. The tax collectors, or publicans as they were known, were corrupt and dishonest. They were Jews appointed by the occupying Roman government to collect various taxes from the people. They were the Internal Revenue Service of the day in the cities and villages around Judea and were well known for extorting more money from the people than what was rightfully owed. The "extra" taxes went into their own pockets. You can understand why these publicans were so despised by the people. They were robbing their own people.

Our friend Zacchaeus was not only one of these nasty tax collectors, but he was the chief tax collector. He was the boss. It is very likely that he not only skimmed money from the people, but in all likelihood he received kickbacks from other crooked publicans. He was the Godfather of his day, the head of organized crime in Jericho, at least as far as the crime of tax extortion was concerned.

But when Jesus saw Zacchaeus sitting high atop the sycamore tree, hoping to catch a glance of the miracle worker of Galilee, Jesus called him to come down out of the tree. He told Zacchaeus that He wanted to be a guest in his home that day. When he heard Jesus' request, he was ecstatic. He must have thought to himself, *This great man wants to visit with me in my house?* He could scarcely believe someone of Jesus' stature would want to have anything to do with a man of his unsavory reputation. He immediately climbed down and accompanied Jesus to his home with great excitement.

But many of the people who heard about this arrangement were not happy about it. In fact, they were indignant. They began to murmur and complain about Jesus wanting to spend time in the home of such a notorious sinner. Surely this was a person to be avoided like the plague because Zacchaeus was certainly not someone with whom any decent person would associate, they reasoned.

But what these murmuring people didn't realize was that while in the company of Jesus, Zacchaeus began to undergo a radical transformation in his life. So much so, that he announced to Jesus and the other guests in his home that he would give half of his wealth back to the poor. He further promised to return money fourfold to people he had cheated as a tax collector.

These were not hasty statements made by someone who just wanted to look good in front of Jesus. This was a genuine change of heart and mind in a man who had become hardened through sin and wrongdoing. Being in the presence of the Son of God changed his life forever. This man may have been hated and despised by men, but not by God.

We must understand that Jesus modeled the will of God wherever He went, and in everything He did. Jesus didn't spend all His time in the synagogues encouraging other devout Jews. Instead, He reached out in love to some of the worst sinners of the day. He deliberately went out of His way to touch those kinds of people. It's interesting that one of the names the Word of God ascribes to Jesus is "the friend of sinners" in Matthew 11:19.

Jesus was not ashamed to be seen with hardened sinners of the day. And you and I cannot be so holy and so spiritual in our own eyes that we fail to show the love of God to people who need it most. Jesus said that we are the light of the world. He went on to explain that light should not be hidden under a basket, but that it should be placed up high so all can see it. We are not to copy the behavior of the world, but instead we are to shine our light—our witness—out where it can do the most good. We are not to just shine before other Christians, but before people in the world who would never think about coming to church.

Do you know where light is needed the most? In darkness. Light is least effective when other light is present. If you take a flashlight outside on a bright sunny day and turn it on, you can barely see it glow. The same principle applies with light and dark in the spiritual realm. Sometimes we only hang out with those who hold the same Christian values we do, and yet, our light shines best in the midst of spiritual darkness where the need for light is the greatest.

Many times we have the notion that all God expects of us is to go to church, sing praises to God, hear another sermon and go home. That's all. Too many Christians think we should just attend church and that in doing so we've done our duty. We punched our timecard at the clock and did our job; we put in our time; we did our duty. But friend, there's already enough light inside the church building. We're called to go to the dark places of this world and allow the light of Christ to shine forth. That's where light is needed the most, and that's where light is most effective.

Many believers pray that the Lord will release them from their place of work because there are too many sinners around them, making them feel uncomfortable. But these are the very people who need our light the most. Instead of asking God to rescue us from all the ungodly folks around us, our prayer should be that our light will shine even brighter. We should ask God to give us fresh fire and a new passion and enthusiasm every day for those we encounter who are lost and desperately in need of the love of God.

We cannot lose sight of the primary reason that we, the Church, are here. Our purpose is not to be chasing after money and things. We're not here to do our own thing. The Bible says, "we are His witnesses" (Acts 5:32). The Church is God's means, His vehicle of making disciples of all nations. Jesus gave His life for the sins of the whole world, not just you and me.

We cannot allow ourselves to become ingrown and isolated from society. We shouldn't fear becoming contaminated by unbelievers. If that had been Jesus' mindset, how could any of us have ever received eternal life? Let's determine to step outside our Christian bubble and reach out to hurting people with love and compassion. If believers everywhere would make the commitment to venture outside the safe comfortable walls of our churches and reach out to sinners, we would witness a tremendous explosion of growth in the kingdom of God. The world would experience real Christianity; the world would see the Church Jesus had in mind.

The last verse of the passage in Luke 19 that deals with Zacchaeus' conversion reads, "For the Son of Man is come to seek and to save that which is lost." I'm well convinced that if Jesus were here today in the flesh, He would make it a point to deliberately go after the kind of people that some folks feel uncomfortable sitting next to in our churches. I am certain after reading the Gospels, that Jesus would eagerly pursue the gang members, AIDS victims, the down and out, drug addicts, alcoholics, the homeless and the prostitutes. And, He wouldn't remind them of what no-good worthless scum of the earth they are. He would not in any way condemn them. He would win them over with love and do His best to restore dignity and value to them.

Jesus would realize, as we should, that at one time all these people were innocent children with no dark past. They were alive unto God, their spirits pure and spotless in God's sight. But as they began to grow up and develop, the nature of sin began to take hold of them; they yielded to wrong temptations somewhere along their way in life. At first their consciences probably bothered them because God was doing His best to deal with them. The Holy Spirit endeavored to convict them of sin and lead them into repentance. But the more they disregarded the Spirit's dealings with their consciences, the more they yielded to temptations. It became easier for them to violate their consciences and before long their once innocent spirits became hardened.

Then, in an effort to fill the empty void inside—the place God should have occupied—they yielded even more to sin and immorality, trying desperately to satisfy the hunger inside their souls. Too many will do anything they can to satisfy the spiritual gnawing deep within them. For some, it's illicit sex; others try drugs and alcohol. Still others become workaholics, hoping that will fill the void. Young people join gangs in an effort to find acceptance and a sense of belonging. Women sell their bodies because they have little or no sense of the dignity and tremendous value God placed on humankind.

Nevertheless, instead of recoiling in disgust over the destructive lifestyle choices many have made, we need to see them as people God loves and wants to salvage from the junk heap of a battered life. God wants to breathe His life and Spirit into them. He longs to rescue these prodigal sons and daughters. He wants to receive them, restore them and proudly display them in His trophy case. God sees them as potential monuments of His love and forgiveness.

I heard a minister recount an incident along these lines that took place several years ago. He explained that he was ministering in a Christian conference in a hotel where he stayed during the meetings. Shortly after he finished addressing the ministers one evening, he went to the lobby and pushed the button for the elevator to return to his room. When the elevator arrived, suddenly its doors flew open and inside were a group of men trying very hard to keep their drunken friend on his feet. As he shared this experience, the minister explained that when he saw this poor soul so intoxicated that he couldn't even stand up, the minister became totally repulsed.

He thought to himself, *How disgusting! That man is making a fool of himself being so out of control in public. How dare he act that way. He should be ashamed of himself.* As this minister thought on these things, still totally disgusted with the actions of the drunk man, the Lord spoke to his heart and said to him, "Son, the only difference between you and him is Me!" You see, left to our own devices and without the grace and mercy of God, where would any of us be?

> It is of the Lord's mercies that we are not consumed, because His compassions fail not. They are new every morning: great is Thy faithfulness" (Lamentations 3:22-23).

God's love is the most powerful force in the world. It has the supernatural ability to transform a life—any life. No one is beyond the reach of the love of God. If it were not for the faithful compassion of the Lord, where would any of us be?

GOD'S LOVE IS THE MOST POWERFUL FORCE IN THE WORLD.

The Word of God does warn us that friendship with the world is enmity or an enemy with God. It goes on to say that he who would be the friend of the world makes himself the enemy of God (James 4:4). Certainly, we are warned against loving the things of the world. But these verses do not mean that we are to steer clear from those who don't know the Lord and refuse to have anything to do with them. It simply means that believers should not maintain intimate fellowship with nonbelievers on a regular basis. But, by all means, we should let our light shine.

Jesus reached out to people of various stations in life: the rich, the poor, sinners, lepers and harlots. Sometimes we have the idea that our reputation and our standing in the church would be tarnished if we were seen in the company of people who live questionable lives. But the irony of this kind of thinking is that Jesus was criticized for doing the same thing.

> But their scribes and Pharisees murmured against His disciples, saying, Why do ye eat and drink with publicans and sinners? (Luke 5:30).

Jesus' reply in the next verse gives us great insight into what our attitudes should be regarding those who don't live godly lives. How should we deal with them? Do we write them off as worthless and keep them out of our churches? Do we avoid being corrupted by them? Should we stay as far away from them as possible? Notice Jesus' attitude toward them:

> And Jesus answering said unto them, They that are whole need not a physician; but they that are sick. I came not to call the righteous, but sinners to repentance (Luke 5:31-32).

Sick people need a doctor. Distressed people need help. Drowning people need someone to throw them a lifeline. The hungry need someone to feed them. The naked need to be clothed. And most definitely, sinners need a Savior. But what they don't need is someone to point out all their faults and condemn them to hell.

Jesus made it clear that His purpose was not to travel from city to city just to bless other believers and celebrate with them in the synagogues every Sabbath. Instead, He went beyond the walls of the house of worship to reach those who needed Him the most. And God is asking us, the Church, to do the same thing. It's not our job to judge people; it's our job to love people. If people want to criticize us for being messengers of God's forgiveness and mercy to the unlovely and despised people in our society, if they want to accuse us of spending time with people who are unwelcome in their churches, so be it. I would rather err on the side of God's love, mercy and forgiveness than I would on the side of judgment and condemnation toward those who need to hear some Good News.

If we are persecuted for adopting this attitude, we're in good company; Jesus was persecuted for the same thing. He was the friend of sinners. Those living outside of the covenant of God should feel welcome in our churches. Our places of worship should be filled with the presence of God and the love of God. People visiting our sanctuaries should experience an encounter with God. When they walk out the church door, they should leave forever changed by the power of God.

There is a world of bruised and shattered people who need the touch of God in their lives. You and I are called to bring the breath of heaven to people who do not normally go to church. The Word of God tells us that Jesus is "the true Light, which lighteth every man that cometh into the world" (John 1:9).

Every person needs the light and the life Jesus came to give. The very people we write off, the very ones we shun are the ones Jesus gave His life to save. God never intended that the church be a museum to display perfect people. He intended that the church be a place where hurting people can be helped. The church was intended to be a place where people can receive restoration, healing, forgiveness and love.

The way the world will recognize us as Christ's disciples is when we allow the same love of God that flowed from Jesus to flow from us. God's love does not see people as they are, but it sees them in light of what God yearns to do in their lives. God's love will reach down to hurting, suffering people and raise them up to live the life they were created to live.

In fact, the Church is made up of those who've been transformed by Love Himself through the New Birth. People just like you and me who've been lifted out of the pit and despair of sin and filled with the life and nature of God. The love of God is what draws people to the foot of the cross to meet the One who created them. Will the real Church please stand up and commit to be fearless carriers of this wonderful, redemptive love?

CHAPTER 7

CHRISTIANITY 'LITE'

I am a certified baby boomer. I was born a few years after World War II ended, during the time when thousands of weary soldiers returned to the United States to resume civilian life once more. Our valiant GIs who fought with gallantry and bravery to rid the world of tyranny returned home to an America that would soon experience massive social and cultural changes.

Fashions would radically change—even automobile styling would take on a futuristic, streamlined look. Popular music was changing as well, and the big band swing would soon give way to rock and roll. Domestic life and work life in the United States also would see a drastic shift. More married women were choosing to work outside the home, something many women were forced to do when they replaced our fighting servicemen in the manufacturing plants during the war years.

Convenience became the driving force in the average American household. In fact, as the 1960s began to unfold, the pace of life stepped up considerably. Life in America changed rapidly; people were in a hurry, and modern life was pacing much faster. Actually progress leaped forward at a dizzying pace; innovation, invention and competition drove the marketplace.

As a society we wanted everything right now: the quicker the better. People didn't have time to sit and wait for food to be cooked, and thus the age of fast food dawned. McDonald's and Burger King were born. In fact, in 1962 the first diet soft drink appeared on grocers' shelves, appropriately called Diet Rite Cola. It was an instant hit with consumers, featuring a no-calorie artificial substance replacing sugar. Soon, American pantries were deluged with foods that boasted reduced calories, reduced fat and reduced carbohydrates. Today, the typical American diet consists of a host of "lite" products, those with fewer calories, fats and carbohydrates.

In much the same way, the landscape of contemporary Christianity has taken on a "lite" quality. We are witnessing a shocking reality in our day. The greatest message ever delivered to mankind—the gospel of Jesus Christ—has, in too many circles, degenerated into what I call "Christianity Lite."

Much of what comes forth from American churches can be compared to spiritual junk food. Pulpits in our churches were once called *sacred desks* because the scriptures were expounded with Holy Spirit power and conviction. Now, in many churches across the land, pulpits have morphed into lecterns or podiums from which pastors espouse the latest winds of popular psychology and faithless liberal theology. Worse yet, this information is disguised as preaching. The truth is, there are far too many messages laced with faithless man-made doctrines and traditions.

Noticeably absent from many modern pulpits is the rightly divided, Spirit-anointed, God-breathed Word that makes men free. In its place are motivational speeches and feel-good messages designed to pander to lukewarm, carnal and half-committed believers filling the pews.

Where have all the preachers gone? Where are the men and women of God with backbones of steel and a holy boldness that compelled them to preach the uncompromising Word of God? Sadly, they have been replaced by life coaches, who expound a gospel of self-help, goal setting, behavior modification and positive thinking instead of simply preaching a Jesus who changes men and women from the inside out.

In the same way that manufacturers have stripped the needed carbohydrates, calories and fats from the foods we consume and have sold us on substitutes of lite food and drink, in many churches the rich, unadulterated Word of God has been stripped of its power. The result is spiritual famine in our churches today. Too many churches are filled with people who suffer spiritual malnutrition. It is no wonder so many Christians faint in spiritual weakness and fall into every conceivable sin and failure.

Friend, God in His unsearchable wisdom included certain healthy fats, carbohydrates, proteins and calories in the foods He created for man to consume. He did so because our bodies cannot function without a certain amount of them on a daily basis. In the same way, God has designed our spirits to require healthful nutrition. He has provided His Word so we can enjoy a robust, dynamic and healthy spiritual life. Within the pages of sacred scripture is found the Creator's manual for profitable and victorious living. The Bible is not a religious book meant to be misconstrued and misquoted in the form of sectarian, denominational creeds and doctrines. It is a book of life to sustain us. The Bible offers instructions from the Master that teach us how to experience the kind of life He had in mind for us to live.

When will the Church realize that God is right about everything? He knows everything about everything—no matter what the topic. God is much smarter than we are by a long shot. In fact, here's something to think about: God has *never* had an idea. He doesn't operate on ideas; He operates in truth. For God to have an idea would mean there was something He did not know beforehand, which is not even possible. There is nothing in all of eternity past, present or future that God does not already possess complete knowledge and understanding about. He is all knowing.

Paul observed that we "see through a glass (or mirror) darkly.... Now, I know in part..." (1 Corinthians 13:12). That means there are parts of God's being and plan that we see, and there are parts we do not yet see. There are things we know, and things we don't know. But God knows everything.

Given the immutable facts concerning God's omniscience, how utterly arrogant and foolish for mere humans to audaciously tamper with and attempt to change the holy things of God and the sound doctrine found in the pages of God's Word. There is a stern and sobering warning given to anyone who would dare take it upon themselves to add to or take away from the revealed Word of God:

> For I testify unto every man that heareth the words of the prophecy of this book, If any man shall add unto these things, God shall add unto him the plagues that are written in this book; And if any man shall take away from the words of the book of this prophecy, God shall take away his part out of the book of life, and out of the holy city, and from the things which are written in this book (Revelation 22:18-19).

Can the Lord possibly make Himself any clearer on the dangers of inserting man's theories, ideas and philosophies in place of His Word? Only a very unwise person would dare supersede God's Word with practices and beliefs that run crosswise with revealed truth in the pages of scripture and not understand the serious consequences associated with such an act. Yet, hundreds of years before the Lord Jesus came to this world to bring the light of redemptive truth to those blinded by spiritual darkness, the prophet Amos warned that the world would experience a famine. The prophet was not talking about a famine of crops, but a drought of hearing, receiving and obeying the words of the Lord.

> Behold, the days come, saith the Lord God, that I will send a famine in the land, not a famine of bread, nor a thirst for water, but of hearing the words of the Lord: And they shall wander from sea to sea, and from the north even to the east, they shall run to and fro to seek the word of the Lord, and shall not find it (Amos 8:11-12).

That is an accurate description of the times we live in today. We have more churches, more ministries, more seminars, more Christian broadcasting than ever before. There are more Christian conferences conducted today than at any time in recent history. To their credit, many ministers are holding forth the Word of Life accurately and powerfully, expounding the mighty, redemptive truths of the Bible in a manner that brings glory to God.

On the other hand, I am dumbfounded at what passes for gospel ministry on many Christian television programs across our nation today. Some of it is absolutely appalling. I have never witnessed such a glut of foolishness, error-riddled, crazy doctrine and downright dishonest business in all my life. There seems to be an endless parade of emotionalism and excess being poured out upon gullible viewing audiences. In many cases, there's a famine of the uncompromised Word of truth in many of these broadcasts.

Some preachers claim to have received a special anointing or a special revelation from the Lord and then make an appeal for offerings to make the revelation available to their listeners.

These preachers will part with the so-called revelation God gave them if listeners will part with their money, that is. Then again, the more money sent to them, supposedly the greater the level of blessing received. Is this a Bible principle? Decidedly not! Whatever happened to the scripture that instructs us "freely you have received, freely give"?

Someone might ask, "Doesn't God still impart special anointings and giftings to ministers today?" Yes, He does. "Does the Lord still reveal Himself to people in supernatural ways today?" Yes, most definitely. Thank God, He does make known His ways and His acts today in special ways as He sees fit. But I promise you that God's purpose in these holy things is not intended to financially enrich a minister operating in these special anointings at the expense of some desperate soul hoping and praying to God for a miracle in his or her life.

Shame on these religious shysters who prey on the desperation of innocent, albeit unwise, people; how unfortunate for those who put their trust in misguided, dishonest preachers instead of in God, who does not fail. I don't know which is worse: ministers who perpetrate Christian con games against needy people or those who unwisely respond to such nonsense, believing that giving their money away will result in a breakthrough in their life.

Certainly not all ministries are guilty of shameful scams disguised as opportunities to receive blessings from the Lord. Yet, in the past few years I've observed too many instances where viewers are assured that God is literally waiting in the wings ready to perform mighty miracles if the one needing the miracle can simply muster up enough faith to "sow your best gift" to the minister making the appeal.

I have yet to hear ministers on these programs promise God's miracles to donors who sow their special miracle offering to their local church. Amazingly enough, God's power to bring a much needed blessing into hurting people's lives can seemingly only come when the offering is given to the ministry hosting the broadcast.

Wake up, Church! Are you as appalled at these troublesome and misleading schemes as I am? Think about it. Where in all the New Testament do you see God's promise to save your loved ones, restore your broken marriage, get you a new and better job, or rain money down on you because you sowed an offering into a ministry? I don't care how impassioned the plea or how much sweat runs down the preacher's face. It matters not how convinced the preacher is that God "spoke to him or her" about the special offering or the benefits God "told" the minister would come to you if you gave. Beware of this sort of thing.

> **WHERE IN ALL THE NEW TESTAMENT DO YOU SEE GOD'S PROMISE TO SAVE YOUR LOVED ONES, RESTORE YOUR BROKEN MARRIAGE, GET YOU A NEW AND BETTER JOB, OR RAIN MONEY DOWN ON YOU BECAUSE YOU SOWED AN OFFERING INTO A MINISTRY?**

I've noticed in many of these spiritual shakedowns that if these preachers attempt to use scripture at all to reinforce their outrageous claims, they nearly always refer to the Old Testament. But, friends, we do not consult the Old Testament to ascertain proper doctrine and practice for today. We live under a newer and better covenant (Hebrews 8:6), and therefore we learn sound doctrine from the New Testament, especially from the Epistles, the letters written to the churches.

I realize it costs a lot of money to broadcast programs on TV and radio. The expenses for Christian broadcasting often are not underwritten by commercial sponsors. I understand that it is up to viewers to choose whether or not to support the TV ministry financially. But that is a choice viewers should be free to make because they truly believe in the ministry and feel led of the Lord to help support it. Spiritual coercion is never an acceptable reason to give an offering.

I've seen Christian networks conduct annual fundraising efforts in order to maintain the programming they offer, and I've been extremely blessed. Testimonies from real people are shared, the ministries the network supports are presented factually and honestly, and the whole thing is permeated by the sweet aroma of the Lord's presence. Thank God for works like these that positively impact people's lives with the Good News of Jesus Christ.

But, regrettably, I've witnessed too many of the other kind of programs where professional fundraising ministers are hired to raise money using some of the most unethical and questionable tactics. They make the most ludicrous claims of God's "miracle" provision you could ever imagine. I believe in many cases these hucksters are counting on the naïveté of many Christians to successfully pull off their schemes and line their pockets with cash.

If God truly called someone to start a Christian TV network, then friend, He is well able to cause the finances to come in to keep the programming on the air. Where God guides, He provides. And He can do so without the spiritual arm twisting so common in some Christian broadcasting circles today. It strikes me as hypocritical that the people who exhort viewers to "believe God for your miracle" cannot themselves do the same thing in regard to the finances necessary to keep their programs on the air. If they truly believe, they can finance their ministry without all the hype and grossly exaggerated promises they feel compelled to make.

The gullibility of Christians in these areas also is troubling. I'm convinced if we spent as much time in our Bibles and on our knees in prayer and communion with God, we would already be experiencing a continual blessing and miracle provision of God, without having to resort to these games of chance. God is so much bigger and so much more reliable and dependable than these shadowy devices of men.

I believe Church leaders have a responsibility before God to preach and teach believers the importance of personal daily devotions, Bible study and prayer. God responds to faith, not to foolishness. If Christians would take it upon themselves to cultivate their own spiritual life and walk of faith, the Church would be much stronger and much wiser in the holy things of God today; believers would not be such easy prey for the enemy to deceive and to disappoint.

Another troublesome issue I've observed in the Church is the tendency of many Christians to get their spiritual feeding and knowledge of the Word from second-hand sources. Too many believers develop their understanding of the Bible through the writings and recordings of their favorite preachers and teachers—not through personal study. They listen to CDs and MP3s, watch Christian-based DVDs and go to their favorite minister's meetings. But unfortunately, for many, these things compose the greater part of their training in God's Word.

Certainly, there are God-called and God-equipped ministry gifts that the Lord has set in the Church to teach and develop the saints. And the advent of recorded media has been a great boon to the Church by providing good faith-building messages that can be listened to over and over again. But these resources were never designed to be the believer's primary source of knowledge and understanding of God's Word; they were designed to *enhance* our personal study not replace our personal study. There's simply no substitute for prayerfully opening up your Bible and asking the Lord to open the eyes of your understanding and relying on the Holy Spirit to disclose great redemptive truths.

Any preacher worth his or her salt will be quick to encourage believers to read and study the Word for themselves. The five-fold ministry gifts that Christ placed in the Church are much needed and used by God to strengthen and equip the Church to do the work of the ministry. But in the final analysis believers must trust the Holy Spirit's ability to lead and guide us into all truth; He is the divine Author of the Bible.

While we have discussed provocative and thought-provoking issues thus far in this chapter, it is not my intention to judge the motives of any man. The fact is, we will all one day stand before the judgment seat of Christ. This is indeed a sobering thought.

And I want to make the point that despite the negative and disturbing trends occurring in the Church world today, there are also many positive, encouraging and exciting things taking place across the landscape of contemporary Christianity. There is a generation of youth poised to take the baton of leadership in the Church who are passionately pursuing Jesus and boldly taking His life-changing message to the ends of the earth. These young men and women have rejected the materialism and carnality so rampant in society today and instead are choosing to focus on living a holy, consecrated and impassioned life for Christ.

These devout young people are introducing Jesus to other youth, many of whom have bought into the lies of popular media selling them the message that popularity and peer acceptance are only possible by engaging in fornication and drug use. Thank God our Christian youth are raising a standard in Jesus that does not march in lockstep to the twisted standards of an ever increasing secular and materialistic society.

There are other positive signs emerging within the Church amid all the other troublesome trends mentioned earlier. We are beginning to witness a great hunger for God and for a mighty outpouring of the Holy Spirit in our land. More than at any time, certainly in my lifetime, we are hearing from many Christians of a greater desire to see God move in our day in great power and demonstration of His glory. Many have the sense that God is about to do something in our time that the world has never witnessed.

There is a heightened sense of expectancy and longing in believers' hearts to see the glory of God in manifestation in our churches and in our nation like never before. Christians in every denomination are growing increasingly dissatisfied with church as usual. They may not be able to fully explain their feelings, but ultimately what they desire is an intimate Bible experience of real fellowship and communion with God. They want to flow in His mighty power more and more. This new breed of young Christians is growing increasingly weary of religion. Instead, they hunger for a deep and abiding relationship with Almighty God. They want to sense the hand of the Lord upon them in every part of their being. They want real Christianity, not Christianity Lite.

The Word teaches us that the whole world is waiting and longing to see the sons of God live up to their calling and begin to manifest the power of God on the earth. The world is waiting for the Church—for you and I—to *be* who we really are, the Sons of God, invested with His very own power and His very own love.

> For (even the whole) creation (all nature)
> waits expectantly and longs earnestly for
> God's sons to be made known—waits for
> the revealing, the disclosing of their sonship
> (Romans 8:19 AMP).

Verse 22 states that all of creation is groaning and in the throes of pain and suffering because of the sin, sickness and death that came into the earth when Adam and Eve disobeyed God. God's original plan was for Adam to be the absolute master of the earth. He empowered Adam with dominion and authority over all the works of His hands until Adam shattered God's perfect creation with an act of high treason. The indescribably beautiful paradise God created for His man now brought forth briars and thorns. Creation became subject to the law of sin and death, and the rebel outlaw Satan became the god of this world.

Everything on the earth was touched by it, and it looked like the devil had won. God's plan was in shambles. Satan had cunningly usurped Adam's authority and death began to reign. Adam and Eve, who once enjoyed rich fellowship with God and walked in unbroken communion with Him, now cowered in fear from God's presence in nakedness and shame. Where life once abounded in God's creation, death soon came to rule.

Actually, the world around us still reels from Adam's disobedience. As we look at the world today and observe the unfolding of alarming events, we see nations in panic mode, and people gripped by fear and confusion. They don't know which is worse—the present distress or the future to come. If you're wondering, *Can things get any worse?* The answer is yes! That is not simply a statement of pessimism. The Prophet Isaiah wrote more than 2,500 years ago that the day would come when people would witness a great spiritual darkness all around them. He foretold of a time when people would be given over to every sort of wickedness and perversion.

Is there any question in your mind that we are witnessing in our day the things Isaiah saw by the Holy Spirit?

> For, behold, the darkness shall cover the
> earth, and gross darkness the people...
> (Isaiah 60:2).

Unrest is widespread in our world today. Hunger, war and the threat of new wars, the specter of radical Islamic fundamentalist terrorism, global economic decline, the development of nuclear weapons by rogue nations are realities that fill our news headlines almost daily. The debasing cancer of pornography is exploding in our society. Lawlessness and iniquity abound. We've witnessed a near total collapse of moral standards in our generation, and the "gross darkness" Isaiah wrote about is right outside our doors. All of these are signs of the times, and there's an unprecedented climate of fear in people's hearts and minds.

So is this a time to wring our hands and lapse into utter hopelessness? Absolutely not. This is the time to lift up our heads and rejoice! Because at the same time darkness and even gross darkness surrounds us, God has promised that we would see His mighty presence upon His people. He's promised that right along with this present evil, we would see the glory of the Lord.

Arise, shine; for thy light is come, and the
glory of the Lord is risen upon thee ... the
Lord shall arise upon thee, and His glory
shall be seen upon thee..." (Isaiah 60:1-2).

As our world plunges into even greater darkness and those around us become engulfed in greater sin and deception, the Word assures us that the Church will be aglow with God's glory and presence. In the same way a beautifully cut diamond shines with brilliance and luster when displayed on a background of black velvet, believers are about to shine with a radiance never before seen in church history. This is the hour for *real* Christianity to be demonstrated—no more half-hearted, watered-down, self-serving Christianity the world has become used to seeing.

How Satan and his evil principalities and powers must laugh with fiendish delight at what we have allowed the Church to deteriorate into over the last centuries. How they must scoff at our pitiful attempts to portray the Christian faith. In Acts the Church was made up of folks who were described as, "those who have turned the world upside down." Rugged men and women of faith willingly sacrificed their lives to introduce Jesus Christ to the uttermost parts of the world. This early band of believers refused to compromise godly principles in order to be accepted by the culture of the day.

They had no interest in being like everyone else. Instead, they challenged and confronted the prevailing status quo. Yet today, unfortunately, we have Church leaders who operate on the premise that we ought to obey man and not God. Of course, this is exactly the opposite approach of the successful Church in the Book of Acts. Nevertheless, many church leaders advise us that our worship services should not be confrontational in any way. Leaders propose that sermons should not be preached or songs sung that might make people feel uncomfortable. Words and phrases like *sin, the blood of Jesus, eternal judgment, hell and the Holy Ghost* must be avoided at all costs, say these so-called experts.

They maintain that this kind of terminology turns people off in our enlightened, modern culture and causes them to feel threatened. Can you believe it? After all, we certainly wouldn't want anyone in our church services to feel anything so passé and outdated as *conviction*, now would we?

How would Jesus respond to this philosophy? Let's look at how He handled confrontation. Jesus was severely reprimanded by the Pharisees on one particular occasion when they learned that He spent time with known sinners. They asked His disciples, "Why does your Master eat with tax collectors and sinners?" When Jesus heard of their questions, He replied, "Sick people need a physician." Jesus' reply underscores a very important point that I believe the present-day Church in America is missing. People need to hear *truth*. People are being destroyed for a lack of biblical knowledge (Hosea 4:6).

The last thing a drowning person needs is a candy-coated pep talk; a drowning person needs a lifeline. The last thing a sick person needs is a motivational speech to cheer him or her up; a sick person needs a physician who can bind his or her wounds. People in trouble need effective intervention, and they need it quickly.

Too many of our churches have drifted from the ancient landmarks established by our spiritual forefathers and pioneers in the faith. God intended that our sanctuaries be places where the holy presence of God lingers in our midst, where the pure sacrifice of praise and worship ascends to the throne of heaven, and God's Word is passionately preached with unction from the lips of preachers totally surrendered to the Lord's will. But, I fear, that too often we're building our churches on activities that will one day prove to have been built of wood, hay and stubble only to be burned up in the fire of God's righteous judgment.

There is a glut of self-promoting, celebrity-minded purveyors mimicking the latest trendy motivational messages in our churches. They drum up themes test marketed to please and tickle the ears of the most carnal, backslidden believer. Some churches and ministries have even resorted to hiring professional public relations firms and marketing consultants to design strategies to attract more people to the churches and to sell more product. Is it any wonder that these kinds of marketing techniques toward church growth have produced perhaps the least committed, most lukewarm, half-hearted believers ever in the past several generations?

IT'S TIME TO ARISE FROM OUR SPIRITUAL SLUMBER, WAKE UP OUT OF OUR COMFORTABLE COMPLACENCY AND BOLDLY CONTEND FOR THE RICH, ROBUST AND LIFE-CHANGING MESSAGE JESUS ENTRUSTED US TO DELIVER.

It's time to arise from our spiritual slumber, wake up out of our comfortable complacency and boldly contend for the rich, robust and life-changing message Jesus entrusted us to deliver. It's time to get back to the full-flavored gospel that exalts the finished, redemptive work of Jesus. It's time to rely on the Holy Spirit to demonstrate the power of God's Word. This is not the time for Christianity lite. God is raising up voices, strong voices, in this hour. The Church is God's vehicle on the earth for the purpose of reaping Him a harvest. Only a Spirit-filled, Holy Ghost-baptized, clean and holy army of God can impact our nation and the nations of the world at this hour. Let's do it!

CHAPTER 8

ANOTHER GOSPEL

> I marvel that ye are so soon removed from him that called you into the grace of Christ unto another gospel. Which is not another, but there be some that trouble you, and would pervert the gospel of Christ. But though we, or an angel from heaven, preach any other gospel unto you than that which we have preached unto you, let him be accursed (Galatians 1:6-9).

There are times when writing to the newly established churches that Paul uses language that is tender, fatherly and filled with deep humility. His approach is that of a concerned father responsible for the spiritual growth of those birthed into the Christian faith as a result of his ministry to them. His words are marked by compassion toward these baby believers as he warns them to be on the lookout for false teachers who would come into their churches like ravenous wolves to destroy God's flock.

Paul shares with these believers that he has wept many tears for them and travailed in prayer that Jesus would be fully formed in them. Yet, in the verses written above to the churches in the region of Galatia, Paul is not hugging their necks and weeping for them. He's pointing his finger at them, breathing fire and issuing a dire warning of swift and certain divine judgment. What issue does Paul address here that unheeded would result in such awful consequences for these believers? Simply this: He levels a warning against preaching any other gospel message than the one Paul already preached to them; more importantly, he warns against preaching a gospel other than the one Jesus Himself preached.

In Paul's view the only other transgression that could elicit such a stern rebuke and dire consequences was the sin of blasphemy against the Holy Ghost. The fact that anyone would be so foolish as to preach another gospel was in Paul's mind sufficient cause to warrant eternal damnation. His language couldn't be any clearer on this point when he said, "let him be accursed."

In particular, Paul was addressing the issue of mandatory circumcision, prescribed by the Law of Moses as a necessary requirement for those desiring to embrace Christianity. This was, of course, a false teaching some misguided and erroneous teachers were putting forth. Paul stoutly refuted this distortion of the true gospel message that basically changed the gospel of Christ into a combination of God's grace coupled with works of the law.

> Knowing that a man is not justified by the works of the law, but by the faith of Jesus Christ, even we have believed in Jesus Christ, that we might be justified by the faith of Christ, and not by the works of the law: for by the works of the law shall no flesh be justified (Galatians 2:16).

The thought that one would attempt to preach any gospel other than the one delivered to Paul by the Lord Himself was enough to evoke a scathing rebuke from the apostle. The essence of Paul's criticism was that any other gospel than the one he preached to them was a phony gospel, a perversion of truth that was not good news at all. It was a poor substitute for the real thing, a miserable counterfeit with no power to save a soul or heal a body.

What some were calling the gospel amounted to a little bit of truth, a sprinkling of works and a great deal of human logic. It was a diluted message that spurned the awesome grace of God, deliberately twisted the truth of Jesus' atoning sacrifice and attempted to turn its adherents back into a religious bondage of Jewish laws and regulations. It may be another gospel, Paul reasoned, but it wasn't *the* gospel.

There is only one genuine, sent-from-heaven gospel revealed in the New Testament and that is the Good News declared with power by Jesus Christ—the gospel that required the ransom of Christ's pure life. It is the message that Jesus referred to as *"this* gospel of the kingdom" (Matthew 24:14). It is this gospel that emphasizes the death, burial and resurrection of Christ and all that His redemptive work accomplished. The gospel that Paul said was "the power of God unto salvation to everyone who believes—to the Jew first and also to the Greek" (Romans 1:16).

The gospel is the complete work of Jesus—more than just Matthew, Mark, Luke and John's account of Jesus' life and ministry on earth. The gospel is the all-inclusive ministry of Jesus, but it's also the sum total of all that Jesus is. It encompasses the entire scope of not only the redemptive work of Jesus, but is also the revelation of the *person* of Jesus. And because scripture teaches that Jesus Christ is the same yesterday and today and forever, the gospel transcends time and creation. All that God performed in the process of restoring fallen man unto Himself through Christ is part of the gospel.

Notice here that the gospel takes into account several aspects of Christ's person and work.

1. HIS ETERNAL NATURE AND PRE-EXISTENCE WITH THE FATHER

The fact that Jesus existed with the Father before His incarnation in a stable in Bethlehem is substantiated many places in scripture.

> In the beginning was the Word, and the
> Word was with God, and the Word was God.
> The same was in the beginning with God
> (John 1:1-2).

Jesus did not come into being when He was born in Bethlehem; that is simply when He took flesh upon Himself. Jesus always existed; He existed in eternity past with God the Father just as He exists with Him now.

2. HIS WORK IN CREATION

Jesus was the active agent in creation and is referred to as the Eternal Word.

> By Him, and for Him all things were created
> (Colossians 1:16).
>
> All things were made by Him; and without
> Him was not anything made that was made
> (John 1:3).

3. HIS INCARNATION AND SELF-EMPTYING

Paul's writings to the believers in Philippians 2:5-11 tell us that when Jesus came to the earth, He chose to empty Himself.

Verse 7 says He voluntarily "made himself of no reputation." The word translated *reputation* is the Greek word *keno,* which means *to make empty, to abase.* This word carries the thought of laying aside something. What was it that Jesus emptied and laid aside when He left heaven and came to earth? It wasn't His divine nature because He continued to be the Son of God all the while He lived on earth. Jesus laid down or emptied Himself of His divine privileges. He freely relinquished the glory He once possessed with the Father even before the world began.

He gave up His divine body and took upon Himself the body of a man, temporarily laying aside His immortality. He also emptied Himself of omniscience, omnipresence and omnipotence. He acquired the limitations of place, knowledge and power, and yet, He did so without ever committing sin, even though as a man He was tempted in every respect just like you and me.

He became subject to the confines of space, time and the material, the three-dimensional world. He freely accepted the possibility of death and the demands and weaknesses of human flesh, just like us. He became hungry and thirsty, just like us. He needed shelter and clothing, just like us. At times, He grew tired and was subject to feelings of sadness, just like us. He wept like us. He had emotions like us—He laughed, He sighed, He groaned. He functioned totally as a human being like us, and yet, He was a man without sin.

4. HIS EARTHLY MINISTRY

Jesus' earthly life of 33 years is part of the gospel. His being born of a virgin, growing up in the home of a carpenter, maturing into a man and developing an earthly ministry that forever changed the world is part of the gospel. Jesus wasn't pretending to be a man; He was, in every respect, a *real* human being who possessed great courage and compassion. Jesus was bold in the face of religious hypocrisy and legalism. He dared to challenge and take to task the religious hierarchy for the abuses and bondage they afflicted on the people. More than anything, Jesus revealed the true nature of His heavenly Father.

5. HIS SUBSTITUTIONARY SUFFERING AND DEATH BY CRUCIFIXION

And they sung a new song, saying, Thou art worthy to take the book, and to open the seals thereof: for thou wast slain, and hast redeemed us to God by thy blood out of every kindred, and tongue, and people, and nation (Revelation 5:9).

And, having made peace through the blood of his cross, by him to reconcile all things unto himself; by him, I say, whether they be things in earth, or things in heaven (Colossians 1:20).

Jesus' sacrificial death on a Roman cross outside the walls of Jerusalem more than 2,000 years ago remains the singularly most important event in history. His vicarious suffering and subsequent death is absolutely central to understanding the gospel. Jesus' death on that rocky outcropping known as Golgotha, a word that in Hebrew means *the place of the skull*, became the pivotal point in all history, occupying center stage for all humanity for all of eternity.

The cross is more than the death of Jesus at the hands of His enemies. It is more than the suffering and the horrors of the extreme torture Jesus endured. The cross involves God, Jesus, mankind and Satan. It is the means by which God in His foreknowledge of man committing an act of high treason in the Garden of Eden, planned to ransom sinful man.

Jesus willingly submitted to the Father's plan whereby He— being all God and all man at the same time—would willingly give His life to pay the price sin demanded. We were *made* the righteousness of God in Christ Jesus because of the cross. Satan, who once wielded the awful power of sin and death over mankind, suffered eternal defeat once and for all because of the cross.

6. THE THREE DAYS JESUS SPENT IN HELL ARE PART OF THE GOSPEL

He (David), seeing this before, spake of
the resurrection of Christ, that his soul was
not left in hell, neither his flesh did see
corruption (Acts 2:31).

And having spoiled principalities and powers,
he (Jesus) made a show of them openly,
triumphing over them in it (Colossians 2:15).

I realize we're dealing with a very controversial issue here. Small wars have been fought over the question of whether or not Jesus went to hell after He was crucified. Some have expressed outrage that such a thing could even be possible, and many theologians and ministers have regarded this teaching as blasphemy against Jesus. But instead of allowing preconceived religious prejudices and emotions to cloud the debate, why not simply allow the scriptures to arbitrate the matter?

Writing in the Psalms, David was often moved in areas of prophetic truth. By the Spirit of God, he was permitted to see future events involving the Messiah, His ministry and His sufferings. Preaching on the Day of Pentecost about the resurrection of Christ, Peter quoted David's writings in Psalm 16 about the resurrection of Jesus.

For thou wilt not leave my soul in hell;
neither wilt thou suffer thine Holy One to
see corruption (Psalm 16:10).

171

Just so we could be sure David was not referring to himself in this scripture, Peter reiterates this same verse in Acts 2:31 and prefaces it in verse 30 with this statement:

> Therefore being a prophet, and knowing that God had sworn with an oath to him, that of the fruit of his loins, according to the flesh, he would raise up Christ to sit on his [David's] throne; He seeing this before [by the Holy Spirit], spake of the resurrection of Christ, that his soul was not left in hell, neither his flesh did see corruption (Acts 2:30-31).

What was Jesus, the holy Son of God, doing in hell? He was taking our place suffering our punishment for three days. If Jesus had not descended to hell in our behalf, every man and woman on earth would inevitably descend there after their death and separation from God. Christ's death was substitutionary, meaning Jesus bore the curse of sin and suffered the penalty of sin in our behalf. Jesus was separated from God so we would never have to be separated, and He bore the curse of the law so we wouldn't have to bear it. Yet, Jesus accomplished something else there as well. He entered the strong man's house (Satan) in order to overcome him and loosed the captives that Satan held there (Luke 11:22).

JESUS WAS SEPARATED FROM GOD SO WE WOULD NEVER HAVE TO BE SEPARATED, AND HE BORE THE CURSE OF THE LAW SO WE WOULDN'T HAVE TO BEAR IT.

After Jesus fully satisfied the claims of divine justice against the sins of man, He stripped Satan of all his authority and power over mankind. He conquered the devil once and for all and took from him the keys, or the authority, of hell and death (Revelation 1:18). And He did it for you and for me. It was as though we personally met Satan on his own turf, engaged him in mortal combat, defeated him, stripped him and dethroned him.

7. HIS RESURRECTION AND ASCENSION INTO HEAVEN IS A PART OF THE GOSPEL

Our redemption was not fully completed until Jesus arose from the dead and then carried His own blood into the heavenly Holy of Holies. There He sprinkled the blood of the everlasting covenant upon the Mercy Seat. This was the consummation of Christ's passion for us, and it was at this point that the human race was declared legally righteous before God. This act gave us a legal right to receive eternal life with Almighty God.

However, this righteousness cannot be enacted and made our own personal possession until we accept Jesus Christ as Savior and confess Him as Lord. When Jesus entered into the heavenly Holy of Holies with His own blood to obtain an eternal redemption for us, the Word of God says that He "blotted out the handwriting of ordinances that was against us ... and took it out of the way, nailing it to his cross" (Colossians 2:14). Through His death, Jesus cancelled the regulations and obligations of the Law held against us because of the weakness of our sinful flesh. He took the evidence of broken laws and commandments in our lives and turned them into a blood-stained receipt stamped "PAID IN FULL."

These seven great Bible truths form the basis of the gospel, which 1 Corinthians 2:7 tells us is itself a mystery hidden in God even before the world.

> Now to him that is of power to stablish you according to my gospel, and the preaching of Jesus Christ, according to the revelation of the mystery, which was kept secret since the world began, But now is made manifest, and by the scriptures of the prophets, according to the commandment of the everlasting God, made known to all nations for the obedience of faith (Romans 16:25-26).

God is not confused or uncertain about the Good News He desires to make known to the world. The gospel discloses God's perfect plan for man, a mystery hidden in God from ages past; a plan that was to be revealed at just the right time through the preaching of the gospel. In fact, the gospel is the vehicle God uses to deliver the news of this wonderful plan to man. You see the elements of these seven great truths of the gospel sprinkled throughout the New Testament. They are taught in the four Gospels, Acts, the Epistles, Hebrews, and finally, in the book of Revelation.

These truths that comprise the gospel are the threads of God's hidden mystery woven together to form a beautiful tapestry of redemption. It is news people all over the world desperately need to hear. It is the message that came to Paul through the direct revelation of Jesus Christ. Paul did not receive this gospel through the teachings of any man on earth. Neither did he receive it from a church, a denomination or a religious organization.

Jesus, the risen Lord of glory, personally taught it to Paul. In fact, Paul embraced this revelation of God's plan for man so readily, grasped it to his bosom so gratefully, and owned it so completely that he called it "my gospel" (Romans 2:16). With that in mind, perhaps, we can begin to understand Paul's righteous anger leveled against those who preached what he called "another gospel." Furthermore, given what Jesus endured in order to offer salvation to the lost and considering the fact that the gospel alone makes salvation possible, any other gospel than the one Paul and Jesus preached becomes nothing less than outright heresy.

Webster's New World Dictionary defines *heresy* this way: "a religious belief opposed to the orthodox doctrines of a church; any opinion opposed to official or established views or doctrines."

There are beliefs and practices taught in American pulpits today that are simply not set forth in the pages of the New Testament. Many church leaders feed people sitting in pews *opinions* that fall woefully short of the truth laid out in the New Covenant. Christian leaders put forth beliefs, practices and doctrines that we never read of Jesus, Peter, Paul or any of the Apostles of the Lamb teaching in the pages of our New Testament.

The scriptures declare emphatically that the Church is built upon the foundation of God's apostles and prophets, Jesus being the chief among them. A building is only as sound as the foundation it's built upon. In other words, it is the rightly divided Word of God received and preached by the apostles, prophets and Jesus Himself that must form the basis of our belief system as Christians. We cannot rest our foundation on trendy new winds of doctrine blowing through the Church that are not clearly taught in the Word and confirmed in the mouth of two or more witnesses in scriptures.

We are living in a time when another so-called gospel is being heralded throughout the land—a poor, powerless substitute for the real thing, a form of godliness that denies the power of God. Much of what we're hearing today is a cheapened message of grace peddled in the marketplace of mass merchandised religion. It is a man-made, man-centered superficial imitation of Bible Christianity that too often fails to drive home the truth of Jesus Christ as the Savior of men's souls, the One who alone forgives our sins, offers eternal life and reconciles sinful man to a loving and merciful God.

In too many churches across America, the pulpit is no longer a place where bold men and women of faith and godly conviction preach the Word of the Lord with a powerful anointing of the Spirit. Too rarely are words preached today that stir the hearts of men and women toward a holy awe of God. Yet in days gone by, preachers delivered messages from heaven that were branded in their hearts by the Holy Ghost. Words that flowed from the preacher's lips came from God's holy presence and a fire shut up in his bones. These preachers pursued their high calling with passion, purity of heart and fidelity to the things of God, and the

Holy Spirit crafted their words and empowered them to address the current spiritual condition of the hearers in the pews.

> UNFORTUNATELY, IN AN INCREASING NUMBER OF PLACES TODAY, PREACHING HAS BEEN REPLACED BY AN ENTERTAINMENT MENTALITY, A MIXTURE OF POP PSYCHOLOGY, MOTIVATIONAL ADDRESSES AND FEEL-GOOD MESSAGES.

Unfortunately, in an increasing number of places today, preaching has been replaced by an entertainment mentality, a mixture of pop psychology, motivational addresses and feel-good messages. Some ministers conduct themselves like cheerleaders, trying to raise the morale of the people by telling them how to feel better about themselves. They encourage listeners to be positive and envision a better life for themselves. These pulpit cheerleaders seek to try to whip the crowd into a state of happy thoughts and optimism.

Instead of undertaking the pastoral responsibility of watching over the souls of the people, guarding and protecting the flock and driving away demon-inspired predators bent on devouring the sheep, many church leaders are driven by self-promotion, success at any cost, the size of their congregations and an unhealthy competitive spirit toward other pastors and churches. This certainly isn't true of all pastors and ministries by any means, but sadly it is true of way too many.

The feel-good messages preached today stand in stark contrast to the gospel that Jesus and Paul preached. In too many instances, it bears little resemblance to the bold, life-transforming message of God's goodness and mercy to sinful mankind. We're missing the simple, yet powerful, message of God's original creation becoming marred by Adam's freewill choice to disobey God, man's subsequent need of a redeemer and Christ's atonement that cleanses us from our sin and gives us eternal life.

Today we are witnessing the preaching of a gospel of accommodation. Yet, the truth of the matter is that the gospel of

Christ is not one of accommodation, but one of confrontation. By its very makeup, the gospel penetrates the innermost being of a person. It makes its way into the hearts and souls of people and forces them to examine their lives and inner motives.

The gospel challenges us, corrects us, and at times, rebukes us. One way or another, the gospel of Jesus Christ gets down inside us and changes us.

> For the Word that God speaks is alive and full of power—making it active, operative, energizing and effective; it is sharper than any two-edged sword, penetrating to the dividing line of the breath of life (soul) and (the immortal) spirit, and of the joints and marrow (that is, of the deepest parts of our nature) exposing and sifting and analyzing and judging the very thoughts and purposes of the heart (Hebrews 4:12 AMP).

What people hear preached from too many pulpits today is not a word from the Holy Bible that exhorts us to passionately pursue a life of purity and absolute surrender to Christ. Rather, people are being exposed to messages that encourage them to pursue their sin and wrongdoing while soothing their consciences. You can live any way you choose. You can sleep around, go to bars and nightclubs, and have sex with as many partners as you choose. You can lie, cheat and steal. And after all this, you can go to a church and hear a nice *nonconfrontational* word telling you that God loves you, and He just wants you to be happy and feel good about yourself.

Friend, do the words you have just read bother you at all? Are you absolutely aghast that this kind of thing is actually taking place inside American churches? Are you shocked, as I am, that we are witnessing God's message of repentance, restoration, forgiveness and reconciliation through the precious blood of Jesus degenerate into feel-good messages that enable folks to live any way they want with no conviction or sense of guilt?

The emphasis of the new gospel being served up in many quarters today is that God wants you to have a healthy sense of self-esteem. The bottom line of this other gospel is that folks leave services feeling right. But I can assure you that God is much more concerned about our being right than our merely feeling right.

You see, the reality is that everybody has something inside them that longs for relationship, a longing to know God and a longing to worship a God who is real.

> Thou art worthy, O Lord, to receive glory
> and honor and power: for thou hast created
> all things, and for thy pleasure they are and
> were created (Revelation 4:11).

It brought God the Father great pleasure in creating us. We were created for a purpose: to worship God, to love and serve Him, and to enjoy an intimate and personal relationship with Him.

Blaise Pascal, a 17th century mathematician, scientist and philosopher, made the following observation about man's inner craving for God:

> What else does this craving and this
> helplessness proclaim but that there was
> once in man a true happiness, of which
> all that now remains is the empty print
> and trace? This he tries in vain to fill with
> everything around him, seeking in things
> that are not there the help he cannot find in
> those that are, though none can help, since
> this infinite abyss can be filled only with
> an infinite and immutable object; in other
> words by God Himself.[1]

Pascal is saying that apart from an intimate relationship with God, we are defective. We don't work right. There is something vital in our lives that is not there; a big piece is noticeably absent. Apart from knowing Him, nothing is really right; we don't think right or act right. It only follows then, that if this void in our life is not filled with God's life, it will have an affect on our feelings. We won't feel right.

This new, nonconfrontational feel-good gospel that is being peddled today works really well for many people whose consciences are salved by simply going to church. But, at the same time, rarely, if ever, are they challenged to confront the reality of their sinfulness and their need of a savior. Believers are not being challenged to live a separated, holy lifestyle. People are being fooled into thinking they are right with God because the bar has been lowered as to what constitutes real, committed Christianity. Don't be deceived by this weak, anemic, powerless message.

This new message of accommodation caters to the carnal, fleshly nature of people. Paul warned Timothy that "in the last days perilous times shall come ... men shall be lovers of pleasures more than lovers of God" (2 Timothy 3:1,4). The Greek understanding of the word *pleasure* in these verses carries the meaning of *sensuous, lustful, self-gratifying sensual pleasure.*

I don't believe there has ever been a time in human history when people have been so consumed with seeking pleasure. The quest for personal gratification, leisure, the preoccupation with sports and entertainment, and other forms of escapism is so prevalent in our culture today. Along with the growth of these acceptable forms of leisure and recreation, we've seen an explosion of the vile and the immoral. The craving for lustful pleasures of the flesh has multiplied exponentially over the past several years. There seems to be no end to the parade of filth and perversion on TV and in the movies. It seems that all norms of decency and propriety have flown out the window.

Sadly, this wickedness and immorality so prevalent in the world has crept into the church. We've watched the downfall of prominent ministers and ministries who failed to exercise moral restraint. Men who once walked in the power and anointing of God's Spirit, bringing messages of salvation, healing and blessing to multitudes, have had their private lives exposed. Their dirty laundry has filled the headlines with reports of adulterous relationships, consorting with prostitutes and homosexual activity.

The divorce rate among believers is as high as those of unbelievers, according to experts who've tracked the numbers of Christian couples over the past decade who have chosen to end their marriage vows. What a tragedy. Is there a remedy? I believe there is.

IT'S TIME TO EMBRACE THE GOSPEL OF THE KINGDOM—NOT A DILUTED, POLITICALLY CORRECT GOSPEL OF ACCOMMODATION.

It's time to embrace the gospel of the kingdom—not a diluted, politically correct gospel of accommodation. The Church must begin to cultivate the same mindset Jesus embodied in these words from Hebrews 1:9, "Thou hast loved righteousness, and hated iniquity...." What compelled Jesus to live this way? Did He simply grit His teeth and reluctantly refuse to sin, even though His flesh really wanted to do it? We must remember that Jesus was tempted in every respect as we are, yet He was without sin (Hebrews 4:15).

Jesus lived close to the heart of God and maintained an ongoing, intimate fellowship with His heavenly Father. He poured out His heart to God on a regular basis. Jesus' prayer life was amazing; He would arise early in the morning before dawn to pray and wait on God. But Jesus' prayer life was not based on a sense of religious duty; it was born out of a great desire to be with His Father. His heart longed for these special, set-aside moments of loving interaction with God.

It was time spent in the holy place of sweet solitude with Abba Father that sharpened His already keen awareness of the destructive nature of sin and iniquity that held the people in an iron grip.

Jesus perceived man's acts of unrighteousness for what they really were: the hideous deception of Satan's strategy to separate mankind from a loving and gracious Father. The last thing the devil wanted was for man or woman, the crown of God's creation, to acknowledge His wonderful plan for their lives.

For this reason, Jesus was moved with compassion to preach and demonstrate a gospel that ministered to those in desperate circumstances. Jesus spoke with a power that made prostitutes pure, a power that caused cheating tax collectors to stop extorting their unfortunate victims. Jesus' words moved a loud-mouthed, impulsive, bitter, mad-at-the-world fisherman by the name of Simon Peter to experience such a total transformation in his life that he became one of the greatest preachers in all of church history.

How powerful is this gospel of the kingdom? It's so powerful that some Jewish religious leaders who initially viewed the gospel as a threat to Orthodox Judaism and the Law of Moses ultimately embraced Christ's message when they realized it did not *deny* the precepts of the Law and the Prophets, but rather the gospel of the kingdom *fulfilled* the law that God delivered to Moses. Sinners willingly embraced the gospel as a message of freedom and deliverance. The sick were healed, blind eyes were opened and the deaf were able to hear once again. Lepers were cleansed and dignity was restored to social outcasts.

What is the real power behind this wonderful gospel? Simply this: The gospel is the revelation of God to hurting, lost and suffering humanity. It is the message the world is waiting to hear. It is not a philosophical discourse. It's not a theory. It isn't even a religion. It is *truth*. It's the way we were intended to live.

It's the only way we function properly. The gospel is the power of God released into the lives of people who believe it, mix faith with it, receive it and allow it to govern their lives.

May the Church throughout the world rise up and throw off the things that have neutralized the awesome power of God's gospel. Let's rightly divide the Word of Truth and give God the opportunity to confirm His Word with signs following. The world doesn't need another movement; it doesn't need another misguided, outlaw religious sect. The world needs to see the real deal. The world needs to hear and see the gospel in action—not another gospel, but the gospel of Jesus Christ.

CHAPTER 9

THE PERILS OF A SLEEPING CHURCH

Wherefore he saith, Awake thou that
sleepest,and Christ shall give thee light
(Ephesians 5:14).

It is clear the apostle Paul is not referring to our need of natural rest and sleep in the above verse. We need the regeneration that only a good night of unbroken sleep can provide our physical bodies. Sleep is necessary to promote good physical health. It restores and revitalizes our bodies and prepares us for the demands that will be placed upon us throughout the day.

Think about what happens when you are fast asleep at night. You become totally oblivious to things taking place all around you in the night. You're in another reality. Your body is in a temporary, suspended state. Animals may be creeping across your yard in search of food. People may be walking down the street in front of your home. Airplanes may be flying in the skies thousands of feet above your house. Breaking news of some great catastrophe in a faraway place may be airing on cable TV, but you aren't aware of it because you are asleep—asleep to the world around you.

The Word of God mentions another kind of sleep that's not good for us at all. In Ephesians 5, Paul refers to a spiritual sleepiness that desensitizes us, a kind of sleep that prevents us from responding to hurting, struggling people with the love of God. It keeps us away from our prayer closet and from intimate fellowship with God. It makes us dull of hearing and slow to respond to God's direction in our lives.

Paul went to great lengths in his letters to the churches to illustrate how our new life in Christ should be reflected in our behavior among people who do not know Christ. People apart from Christ's love are living in a state of spiritual darkness. We shouldn't be shocked by the things sinners do. As we explained earlier, they are simply acting out of their spiritual nature, which is the nature of death. Paul carefully draws a parallel between the vile deeds of unregenerate people and the fruitful works of righteousness that should be the hallmark of every child of God. He further drives home the truth that the godly behavior of believers is not something that occurs automatically in our lives. Paul carefully points out that Christ-likeness is something that must be cultivated in our lives. There must be a continual yielding to the promptings of the Holy Spirit and a willingness to give place to the law of faith and love in order to allow the light of Christ's love to be seen in and through us.

> **THERE MUST BE A CONTINUAL YIELDING TO THE PROMPTINGS OF THE HOLY SPIRIT AND A WILLINGNESS TO GIVE PLACE TO THE LAW OF FAITH AND LOVE IN ORDER TO ALLOW THE LIGHT OF CHRIST'S LOVE TO BE SEEN IN AND THROUGH US.**

Again, Paul dealt with this same issue of spiritual slumber in the 13th Chapter of Romans:

> And that, knowing the time, that now it is
> high time to *awake* out of sleep: for now is
> our salvation nearer than when we believed.
> The night is far spent, the day is at hand: let
> us therefore cast off the works of darkness,
> and let us put on the armor of light. Let us
> walk honestly, as in the day; not in rioting
> and drunkenness, not in chambering and
> wantonness, not in strife and envying. But
> put ye on the Lord Jesus Christ, and make
> not provision for the flesh, to fulfill the lusts
> thereof (Romans 13:11-14).

Paul expresses concern here that some Christians were acting just like the heathen all around them in Rome; they were living like unsaved people who didn't know the Lord. Rome was the epicenter of the great Roman Empire, a city known for wicked and idolatrous behavior.

Every imaginable sin of the flesh was committed by Rome's citizens. Sexual sins, perversion, and homosexuality were considered normal and accepted practices of the day.

But when people are surrounded by these ungodly lifestyles and exposed for long periods of time to them—as wicked as they are—it becomes easier to simply look the other way. If we as Christians fail to guard our hearts and maintain a holy walk with God, we can become mired in what Paul calls the darkness of spiritual slumber. When this happens, we become blind to things that should grieve our hearts and arouse a healthy sense of righteous anger within us.

Believers are instructed to be sober minded and vigilant in several places in scripture. We're not to be asleep to the things happening around us. Instead, we're to be fully awake and aware of the times and seasons of life. Our responsibility as sons of God is to be alert and watchful. Like good soldiers, we need to be standing at attention, keenly observing the unfolding of events, and tuned into the spiritual realities of the day. We're not to be spiritually sleepy and unaware of Satan's strategies to deceive and to destroy. Our mandate as the Church is to be awake, alert, at our posts and prepared to resist the onslaught of our adversary at every turn.

Nevertheless, much of the Church is asleep, living in a perpetual state of apathy and comfortable complacency. Satan, as a roaring lion, is walking about devouring lives and wreaking havoc in families, in churches and among our young people. He's sucking the life out of the moral and spiritual fabric of our beloved America.

It's time for us to wake up! We've been lulled to sleep and into a state of spiritual inertia by a prevailing culture of entertainment, leisure and the empty pursuit of self-centered distractions of modern life. It has marred our focus and crippled our effectiveness as soul winners. We must be willing to put an end to our aimless spiritual sleepwalking and realize the seriousness of the times. The Church must be like the people of Issachar, one of the 12 tribes of Israel. It was said they were people who were wise and who "had understanding of the times, to know what Israel ought to do" (1 Chronicles 12:32).

God is counting on the Church in this generation to know what we ought to be doing. We are to be aware of the wiles of the enemy and raise a mighty standard of resistance against him by boldly preaching the gospel of the kingdom with Holy Ghost power and fire from heaven. We are not here by chance or coincidence. As it was said of Queen Esther, you and I have been brought into the kingdom for such a time as this.

Face the facts. A sleeping church is a powerless church. A sleeping church is an ineffective church; it's one that has allowed the weapons of our warfare—God-given weapons—to become neutralized and rendered useless by a careless indifference and lack of use. A church that is asleep can never reach desperate humanity with the Good News. The masses of suffering and dying people can be rescued only by strong, well-equipped and bold legions of blood-washed believers fully surrendered to Jesus Christ. The great numbers of lost and perishing people will never learn of God's plan for their lives from a weak, carnal, self-absorbed, lukewarm church.

We in America have so many churches; even in the smallest towns one can usually find many denominations represented. Christians dutifully make their way to church on Sunday mornings to join in an ongoing ritual of hymn singing, giving offerings and listening to pastors' sermon. But are we being challenged to go forth from the church building empowered by the Holy Spirit to take a Living Christ to the people near us? Isn't this the mission of the Church? Aren't we Christ's witnesses? Isn't Jesus counting on us to testify of His love to those who need it the most?

As believers, this is our "job description." Too often, though, we Christians are huddled in our church buildings praying for revival. It's good to pray for revival. In fact, a careful study of the history of revival down through the centuries will show that God responded to the heartfelt, earnest prayers of His people by sending a spiritual awakening to the nations. But, dear friend, revival does not come merely by praying.

Many of our notions about revival are so misguided. Do we think some spectacular, supernatural event will occur on earth to capture the attention of people and cause another Great Awakening? The truth is, revival comes when fully committed Christians decide to give all they have to proclaim the gospel. Spiritual awakenings were able to shake nations when God's people placed the highest priority on the things of God and gave themselves completely to Him. But a sleeping church will never be in the center of revival.

Jesus bluntly and forcefully addressed the subject of a sleeping church in the Book of Revelation. Consider carefully the words Jesus spoke to those in the church at Sardis. And keep in mind that even though John received this vision of Jesus during his exile on the Isle of Patmos and penned these words in the first century, Jesus' words of rebuke were leveled against a New Testament church. The substance of what He said to believers in Sardis is relevant and pertinent to the church today.

> ...I know all the things you do, and that
> you have a reputation for being alive—but
> you are dead. Wake up! Strengthen what
> little remains, for even what is left is almost
> dead. I find that your actions do not meet
> the requirements of my God. Go back to
> what you heard and believed at first; hold
> to it firmly. Repent and turn to me again...
> (Revelation 3:1-3 NLT).

Sardis was a rich and powerful city in the ancient world and the capital of Lydia, which had its beginnings in the fifth century B.C. It was situated at the junction of the main royal highways that linked Ephesus, Smyrna and Pergamum. All these cities are mentioned in Revelation chapters two and three because of the churches located there. The city of Sardis was built on top of an extremely high cliff. Today, the Acropolis, the ancient remains of that once great city, sits atop a sheer cliff face on three sides, rising to a height of nearly 1,500 feet. The city was only accessible on the south side of the cliff. It is believed, however, that in the sixth century B.C., this south-facing cliff was much higher than it is presently.

The popular thinking was that Sardis was impregnable and that no army could breach the natural defenses of the cliffs. The citizens of Sardis had lived there in safety for more than 150 years. But in 549 B.C., the Medes attacked the city after climbing the cliffs at night. This was quite a daring gamble that placed the marauding soldiers at great risk. They were easily vulnerable to a deadly barrage of arrows or large boulders hurled by defenders above guarding the city walls.

And yet, when they made their way to the cliff tops and scaled the city walls, they were met with no resistance whatsoever. Sardis had become so confident of her safety and security, their citizens didn't even take the precaution of posting a sentry atop the city walls. The city was sleeping and was caught totally off guard. Sardis fell easily in the surprise night raid. In the final analysis, its people paid little attention to the possibility that there may have been a vulnerability or weakness that needed to be strengthened.

What a very important lesson for us. Take note! When we fail to guard and maintain the really important things in life, we can soon find ourselves—like the people of Sardis—overcome by an enemy and subject to serious consequences.

At the end of the first century, there was a strong church in Sardis. But, unfortunately, the church had grown rich and complacent; the believers lived in the same manner as the other people. Rather than confronting, challenging and positively influencing the worldly culture of their city, the church had been lulled into spiritual slumber. One couldn't tell the believers from the pagans. The church allowed the prevailing culture of the city to snuff out the believers' light and weaken their witness of the power and life of Christ.

When Jesus appeared to John, giving him these strong words of rebuke against the church at Sardis, it was clear that the majority of believers allowed their faith and devotion to Christ to become compromised. They were so much like the heathen in Sardis, that apart from a few believers in their fellowship, they were a church *in name only*.

What a scathing indictment. Here was a Church that once enjoyed a great reputation, but the believers' actions and lifestyle no longer reflected the glory they once walked in. This was a church that was once alive, but had fallen asleep. Jesus was telling them to wake up. Many of our Western churches are in the same condition. We are asleep. Worse yet, we don't even realize it.

It's time to awaken, shake ourselves, repent and be about our Father's business. Jesus told this sleeping church in verse 2 to not only wake up, but also to "strengthen the things which remain, that are ready to die: for I have not found thy works perfect before God."

Apparently these believers were guilty of many of the same things that plague many of our churches today. They had neglected to maintain a vital, intimate relationship with God. Their spiritual life was fading quickly and was almost at the point of extinction. They mirrored in many ways our contemporary "seeker-friendly" church model. They lacked real heavenly dynamism. They were no longer consumed by the fire of the Holy Ghost. Their passion for Jesus Christ had dwindled away and was replaced by a mere religious formality.

The Sardis church started out well, but it lost its holy fire, cooled off and became sophisticated. It moved away from the basics of faith and loving Jesus and became more formal than fiery. The congregation began to focus more on blending in and being accepted by the citizens of Sardis.

But even in the midst of its failings and shortcomings, Jesus still loved this church. Instead of writing it off as hopeless, He gave it the cure for the spiritual sleeping sickness. The greatest need was to strengthen the little flame of godliness that did remain. This sleeping church needed to wake up. In order for that to take place, the spiritual remnant that remained had to once more focus on the basics of the Christian faith. This once great church needed once again to concentrate on core essentials like evangelism, missions and the discipleship of new believers. It needed to emphasize the things Jesus taught His first disciples—being rooted and grounded in the Word of God and the ministry of the Holy Spirit. The people needed to be constantly reminded that the gospel is the power of God.

Knowing these things and practicing them will make any church wide awake and powerful. A church like this will be a mighty force in heralding the gospel and delivering people from darkness. A church that is awake, alive and energized by Jesus will not be mired in the enemy's strategies of sin and spiritual lethargy, but will be a church filled with overcomers.

Jesus reminded the sleepy church of Sardis that if it heeded His warnings, it would overcome and prevail against Satan. No longer would its power become neutralized by compromise and sin, but the church would then be a force with which to be reckoned.

> A CHURCH THAT IS AWAKE, ALIVE AND ENERGIZED BY JESUS WILL NOT BE MIRED IN THE ENEMY'S STRATEGIES OF SIN AND SPIRITUAL LETHARGY, BUT IT WILL BE A CHURCH FILLED WITH OVERCOMERS.

What should shock us and make us weep is seeing so many Christians living in carnality and yielding to the same lusts and temptations that snare unsaved folks. The Word of God clearly teaches that one who calls himself a disciple of Jesus Christ is one who is responsible for maintaining a holy walk with God. Notice how many times the Bible uses phrases like, "Take heed unto yourself, keep your heart with all diligence, be sober, be vigilant, be ye holy even as I am holy." It is up to us to guard our hearts and maintain fervor for the Lord.

Yet, much of what comes forth from church leaders today actually encourages the kind of believer who's easily deceived and misled. We are inundated with teaching that emphasizes how we can become more successful and more blessed. There's an endless stream of TV and radio preachers tickling people's ears, but not feeding hearts and souls. Many of these messages move people emotionally, but rarely move them to repentance or create a desire to live fully surrendered lives to the Lord. Too often these messages are designed to increase audiences and mailing lists, but do they result in an increase of fruitfulness in the kingdom of God?

Paul's words of warning to his son in the faith, Timothy, are as applicable today as they were when he wrote them several centuries ago.

> Preach the word; be instant in season, out of season; reprove, rebuke, exhort with all longsuffering and doctrine. For the time will come when they will not endure sound doctrine; but after their own lusts shall they heap to themselves teachers, having itching ears; And they shall turn away their ears from the truth, and shall be turned unto fables (2 Timothy 4:2-4).

The great apostle who penned these words in his epistle written from prison contains the antidote for a sleeping church: Preach the Word. Awaiting execution for the "crime" of preaching the resurrection of Jesus Christ, what is it that consumes the heart of this great man of God? What final advice does he share with Timothy? Does he tell him to organize a church growth conference in Antioch? Does he tell him to assemble the pastors and teach them the latest marketing techniques on how to have successful churches? Does Paul encourage Timothy to learn all he can about the importance of studying demographics, new technology, Powerpoint presentations and the importance of high-energy contemporary Christian praise and worship? There is certainly nothing wrong about making use of current technology to advance the gospel; we ought to use every available voice we can to preach Jesus.

But Paul's years of rich ministry experience was distilled in three simple words: Preach the Word. He didn't recommend public relations gimmicks, no winds of doctrine, no new revelation. He simply said to preach the Word. Paul knew that a church faithful to proclaim and to live God's Word would never be a sleeping church. He knew a church that was not ashamed of the gospel is one God could work through to awaken and redeem people out of their sins.

> Behold, I stand at the door, and knock: if
> any man hear my voice, and open the door,
> I will come in to him, and will sup with him,
> and he with me (Revelation 3:20).

Very often this scripture is used in an attempt to persuade non-believers to receive Jesus. Of course, we know that Jesus wants to make His life available to anyone willing to acknowledge Him as Lord. But when Jesus spoke these words to the apostle John on the Isle of Patmos, He wasn't beckoning unbelievers to open the door of their hearts and receive Him. In the proper context of Chapter 3, it is clear that Jesus is knocking at the door of a backslidden church in Laodicea. He's standing outside the door of the church, knocking and asking to be allowed back inside His church!

It is a sad indictment, but nevertheless, Jesus is still an unwelcome guest in many churches today. Many of our great churches were once aglow and burning with the Holy Spirit and actively involved in carrying out the Great Commission. But over time they became warehouses of lifeless religiosity. They maintain a form of godliness, but in reality their practices reveal that they have denied the power of God in their meetings. All that is left, in many cases, is an empty form with no real power from heaven to transform people's lives.

It's time for the Church to wake up out of such powerless slumber. We must be willing to repent and once more allow Jesus to take center stage in our congregations. The Holy Spirit must be welcome in our midst again. When that happens, the fresh, refining fire of the Holy Spirit will fall once more. But, sadly, many have been enticed by the enemy's deception and merely go through the motions of church instead of *being* the Church Jesus purchased with His own blood.

This is not a time to be involved in a religious game, doing our own thing while people perish and slip into eternal torment. There are too many believers asleep at the wheel, too many cold, lifeless churches in our land. So much of the Church is either asleep or intoxicated with the spirit of this world. Many are caught up in mindless materialism, selfish pursuits and a me-centered existence that extinguishes our zeal to carry out the Great Commission.

The Church was never designed to be a social club where lukewarm believers give lip service to Jesus Christ while refusing to obey His commands. The Church was never intended to stay safely hidden behind enemy lines while its members privately rejoice in their Christianity. Instead, we are called to emulate the young shepherd boy David and be willing to boldly take the battle to Goliath. In far too many segments of the modern church, believers are like the armies of Israel. They play it safe, crouching down in the battlefield trenches while David, outraged by the coarse boasting and intimidation of the pagan Goliath, rose up and ran *toward* the enemy.

Where are the Davids of this generation? Those who are not content to retreat in safety inside the church building singing songs of deliverance, but never taking that deliverance to those who need it the most. David was not willing to sit idly by, waiting for someone else to do something about this enemy bent on destroying the people of God. David took the initiative and marched toward the Philistine, full of faith. His confidence was rooted in a God whose anointing came upon him through the prophet Samuel when he anointed young David with oil. David understood that this power from God rested upon him in order to deliver people from the power of the enemy.

Does the church today understand the purpose for God's anointing? Are we aware that God has empowered us with His presence and anointing so that people who are burdened with sin, sickness, disease and poverty can be set free? I understand that fellowship with other believers is a rich and wonderful aspect of our Christian life. I realize how important it is that we be strengthened and encouraged as we share our faith and love with one another. But the church is not simply a place where we meet to have a good time with other believers. The Church is a training center for God's mighty men and women, a command hub to prepare and equip us for spiritual war. The church is meant to be a place where we unite with one heart, one mind and one purpose to preach the gospel to every creature.

It has been my privilege to travel to many places and minister the Word to many of God's precious people. They listen intently and receive the Word with great joy. Many later testify how the message they heard helped and encouraged them, and it always blesses me to know that God has used me to be a vessel of refreshing to bring a timely word to the church. But still, one thing is missing in the lives of many folks where God has sent me. They must take the Word they heard, and step out in faith and put into practice what they've heard. They need to be doers of the Word and not hearers only.

You see, a sleeping church is one that hears the Word but fails to act upon it. Listening to the Word being preached is like eating a good meal. You get full and feel satisfied. But in a spiritual sense, when we hear the Word, our hearts get full of spiritual nourishment. The Word is supposed to feed us. But unlike natural food we eat, this Word that fills and satisfies us is to be shared with others. We are to get full of God's truth and then share it with those who are spiritually hungry, so they too can know the goodness of God.

If we keep God's Word and His blessings all to ourselves, we become overstuffed and spiritually lethargic. Just like eating a nice Thanksgiving meal, we become sleepy afterward. But when you share the spiritual food God gives you with others, He will give you more. Friend, there are so many people who need to hear what you and I already know about the goodness of God. I'm convinced the reason many believers today lack joy and feel unfulfilled is because they have allowed the Holy Spirit to dwindle down into barely glowing embers in their lives.

They're overfed and under exercised. If they would step out in faith and boldly share the love of Jesus, their lives would change dramatically. God would begin to use them in a mighty way to bring the miracle of the New Birth to others. No longer would these frustrated believers live under a cloud of discouragement and emptiness. The best way for a believer to get rid of depression, loneliness and boredom is to reach out and touch others with the love of God. Get busy *being* a blessing to others instead of seeking to *be blessed*, and God will give you so much you won't be able to contain it.

Satan, our adversary, is pulling out all the stops, doing all he can to take as many people to hell as he can. There's a great struggle taking place all over the world between the forces of good and evil. The devil's fury is as intense as perhaps no other time in history, and many souls are being swept away into eternal darkness. God's people must be busy about their Father's business. This is the only answer to the demonic warfare being waged against the human race.

God must have an enlightened and energized generation of saints today walking in the spirit and power of John the Baptist who cried out, "Prepare the way of the Lord. Make room in your hearts for a God who is more than enough." The Lord needs men and women of faith like John who are not ashamed of the gospel, those who fear no man. But instead, millions of Christians are asleep and ignoring the lost all around them.

It's time to wake up! It's time to prepare ourselves for the greatest ingathering of souls into God's kingdom ever in the history of man. This is the time for a great harvest to be reaped for the Master. If you ever lived on a farm, especially years ago when it was time to harvest the crops, you know that every member of the family was needed to bring in the harvest. There was no sleeping in during harvest time. All hands were needed, and everything that did not involve reaping the crops was temporarily put on hold. Why? Because there was a small window of opportunity to reap the grain and get it into the barns. The harvest was too precious to lose. There was no time for rest or leisure until the harvest was gathered. In the same way, we must realize God wants a harvest. He is waiting for it, and He's earnestly expecting it.

> Be patient therefore, brethren, unto
> the coming of the Lord. Behold, the
> husbandman waiteth for the precious fruit
> of the earth, and hath long patience for
> it until he receive the early and latter rain
> (James 5:16).

The fruit mentioned in this verse refers to people for whom Christ gave His life to redeem. In the mind of God, their souls have already been ransomed from the penalty of sin by the precious blood of Jesus. But they cannot take advantage of their redemption if they don't know they've been redeemed. Somebody has to tell them this Good News. That's why we are here on earth. God wants what He has already bought and paid for, so let's wake up and determine to get involved in the harvest. It's time to get out of the bleachers of life and move onto the playing field and get into the game. No more spectator Christianity! The real action is on the field, not in the seats.

There are multiplied millions of people professing to be Christians in our world today. But if that is the case, then why are there still so many areas of our world still lying in the grip of spiritual darkness? Why are so many still unreached and untold?

The problem may have something to do with our notions of what Christianity is and how the majority of believers practice their faith. For too many people, serving the Lord is little more than a small compartment of their weekly life, an obligation they occasionally perform on Sundays out of a sense of duty. Going to church is like going to their jobs—like punching a time clock. They show up and put in their time. For others church has become a social gathering where friends hang out, sing a few songs and listen to another sermon. That's it; they've punched the clock and fulfilled their obligation. But where is the passion? Where is the joy?

Many people don't know the real Jesus. Too often in churches today He's being presented as a historical Jesus who died on a cross and a future Jesus who will return some day. But in the vast majority of churches, Jesus is not preached as a Living Christ who powerfully dwells in the hearts of believers, enabling men and women to do the same works in our day that He did in His. Instead, millions of believers are bound up in legalism and dead formality, plodding along, routinely marching in lockstep to man-made rules and traditions.

Instead of walking with the Master, enjoying a relationship of love and friendship with Him hour by hour, too many Christians treat Him as some heavenly being millions of miles away. Friend, if you have been living your Christian life this way, I have news for you: Jesus is the best friend you'll ever know in this life and in the life to come. He lives in your skin! He wants you to take His outstretched hand and walk with Him through this life, doing great exploits together!

Don't allow your Christianity to become a weary endurance test. If your experience as a believer has been one of boredom, unfulfilled expectations, tired and worn out rituals, and little joy, then you're not doing it right. When we walk with Jesus the way He instructed us to, there's joy unspeakable and glory!

Don't be like Lazarus. Lazarus died prematurely at a young age. Jesus came to Bethany, where Lazarus was buried, when He heard the news of his death. But Jesus was not content to let

His friend remain dead. He called Lazarus out of the tomb, out of death. To everyone's astonishment, the dead man walked out of the grave. But even then, once out of the tomb, Lazarus still had grave clothes wrapped tightly around his body. He was alive, but he was bound. Taking note of his condition, Jesus said, "Loose him, and let him go."

Many have experienced the New Birth, but they remain bound—bound in sin, bound in habits, bound up in dead religion. They, like Lazarus, need to be set free. Jesus didn't want to see Lazarus merely live again; He wanted Lazarus to be free. Jesus gave His life so every man and woman could be free.

> A CHURCH THAT IS BOUND UP IN MONOTONOUS RELIGIOUS ACTIVITIES, AND BOUND UP IN LEGALISM AND TRADITIONS OF MEN WILL NEVER BE A CHURCH THAT TURNS THE WORLD UPSIDE DOWN LIKE THE ONE IN THE BOOK OF ACTS.

Don't be deceived. A church that is bound up in monotonous religious activities and bound up in legalism and traditions of men will never be a church that turns the world upside down like the one in the book of Acts. But the world will respond when it sees Christians who are the real thing. The world must see a church that's awake and pulsating with the life of the risen Savior.

Wake up sleeping Church!

CHAPTER 10

UNCONDITIONAL SURRENDER

Bringing to a close the bloodiest war in human history, President Harry S. Truman announced on August 15, 1945, that Emperor Hirohito of Japan had fully surrendered all of the military forces of the Empire of Japan. The fighting between Japan and the United States in the Pacific theater of World War II had finally ended.

Wild celebrations in cities around the world paved the way for the fateful day of September 2, when a huge force of Allied ships assembled in Tokyo Bay for the signing of the peace treaty. Aboard the battleship USS Missouri, official documents outlining the terms of peace were signed by officials representing the Empire of Japan and by Gen. Douglas Mac Arthur representing the government of the United States.

The treaty was signed because Japan was forced to surrender its military forces and admit defeat—the country had no other choice. By August 1945, Japan was in a desperate situation. Its major cities were in shambles in the aftermath of both conventional and atomic bombings. Civilian casualties numbered in the millions. Vast numbers of citizens were reduced to refugee status and food was in short supply. The Japanese naval fleet was all but destroyed. Merchant shipping used to transport food and much-needed supplies was at a standstill because Allied naval forces surrounded the coast of Japan. Oil stocks were depleted. War material so necessary to carry on the battle rapidly dwindled.

Japan was a defeated nation and clearly the time to surrender had come. Any other nation suffering these same desperate circumstances would have surrendered much sooner, so why did the emperor wait so long? What was his rationale for allowing the prolonged suffering and the mounting death toll before his inevitable surrender?

At the foundation of the emporer's reluctant decision was the Japanese mindset that surrender is not an option. This creed was developed over centuries of Japanese warfare dating back to the famed samurai warriors. It was the ultimate display of dishonor for a Japanese warrior to lay down arms and admit defeat—an extreme act of cowardice and disgrace. Instead, when defeat appeared unavoidable, ancient warriors chose suicide as more honorable than surrender.

Surrender is an unpopular word in our modern vernacular, and another equally abhorred word is *submission*. To most people, both imply weakness and defeat; both words evoke images of losing. We don't want to lose; we want to win. Winning is everything. In today's highly competitive culture, we are taught to never give up. In fact, we hear very little today about the virtues of surrender. If winning is everything, surrender is unthinkable. In the Western world, we hear endless sermons based on the theme of winning, success, conquering and overcoming. And friend, there is no question that walking with Jesus enables us to live in victory. But there seems to be a noticeable absence of messages that deal with the subject of yielding and surrendering to the Lord.

The irony in all this lies in the fact that surrender is at the very heart of the Christian faith. Jesus Christ, the central figure and object of our faith, fully surrendered to the will of God. There never was a time in His life when Jesus was not completely sold out to the will of His Father.

> Let this same attitude and purpose and
> [humble]) mind be in you which was in
> Christ Jesus: [Let Him be your example in
> humility:] Who, although being in essentially
> one with God and in the form of God
> [possessing the fullness of the attributes
> which make God God], did not think this
> equality with God was a thing to be eagerly
> grasped or retained; But stripped Himself
> [of all privileges and rightful dignity], so as
> to assume the guise of a servant (slave),
> in that He became like men and was born a
> human being. And after he had appeared in
> human form, He abased and humbled Himself
> [still further] and carried His obedience to
> the extreme of death, even the death of the
> cross! (Philippians 2:5-8 AMP).

No one has surrendered to God's will and purpose as completely as has Jesus; He remains the greatest example of godly surrender in all the Word of God. And, in doing so, Jesus left us an example that we as His disciples are required to emulate. Simply stated, the Christian life is a life of total commitment— submission and surrender—to God and to His ways.

But what is true surrender? It is the heart's response to God's unconditional love and mercy that He freely and willingly lavished upon us. Even though we as fallen creatures deserve punishment and judgment for our sins, surrender is our response to His love. We give ourselves to Him not out of a sense of fear or rigid duty, but out of love. Why? Because He first loved us (1 John 4:19).

True worship begins when you give yourself completely to God; it is the act of offering yourself unconditionally to the One who loved you before you were ever born. You see, God wants you to surrender all your life to him, not part of it. Ninety-five percent is not enough. Surrendering most of your life will not cut it. Think for a moment how different your life would be today if Jesus had given *most* of His life for you. What if He had not been quite ready to trust the Father enough to surrender His whole life? We would still be lost in our sins without hope and without God.

Surrender is an ongoing process in our lives; it's a journey and not a final destination we achieve. Salvation, or the initial act of surrender to Jesus, was just the starting point in your journey with God. The truth is, you will never know real joy, peace or fulfillment until you learn what it means to live a fully yielded life. Choosing the pathway of surrender will transform your perspective and revolutionize your life. It is the *only* way you can become conformed to the image of Jesus Christ and be like Him.

Too many believers are content with giving God some of their life. They don't mind if the Lord deals with them about rearranging some of their priorities and practices. But we need to realize that total surrender to God is the only path to a fulfilling and rewarding life. True surrender is not a painful, difficult sacrifice we make as we grit our teeth and lament all that we have to give up in order to please the Lord. Rather it is an obvious response to the Lord who was willing to give up everything for our sakes.

That is why Paul called himself a *bondservant*. The Bible also uses the word *bondslave*. What is a *bondslave*? It's one who's in subjection to another, but without the idea of being in cruel bondage because of it. It is closely related to the idea of being *bound* to another willingly, not out of forced compulsion.

It is important to understand that when we were born again, we entered the School of Surrender.

> What? know ye not that your body is the temple of the Holy Ghost which is in you, which ye have of God, and ye are not

your own? For ye are bought with a price:
therefore glorify God in your body, and in
your spirit, which are God's (1 Corinthians
6:19-20).

How I wish this scripture were preached today from every pulpit in America. Although its message may be new to many, it is absolutely vital to realize that if you are a Christian, you are not your own. Someone else owns you. Somebody bought you. Another person has a claim on your life. You don't belong to you; you belong to God. You are now in the glad position of being the personal, purchased possession of Almighty God. In fact, He loved you so much He bought you when you were a mess.

We have all shopped in stores and noticed that certain merchandise had a price tag attached to it that read *as is*. What does the phrase *as is* mean? It means that if we choose to buy this particular piece of merchandise, we do so with the understanding that it's not perfect. There are flaws and imperfections associated with it that makes it less valuable than an item of first quality.

The good news is, when God purchased us—not by corruptible things such as silver or gold, but by the spotless, precious blood of Jesus—He bought us as is, defects and all. Even though we were full of blemishes and imperfections and dead in trespasses and sins, God saw something in us worth salvaging. The reality is, when we came to Christ to receive salvation, we became Christ's very own possession. And He wants *all* of what He bought and paid for—not just some of us. As we learn to joyfully yield to Him on a daily basis in loving trust and obedience, the rewards in our lives will be incomparable.

There is a concept mentioned many times in the Old Testament that has to do with the "jealousy" of God. He is even referred to as a *"jealous God."*

For I the Lord thy God am a jealous God
(Exodus 20:5).

For the Lord, whose name is Jealous, is a
jealous God... (Exodus 34:14).

...For the Lord thy God is a consuming fire,
even a jealous God (Deuteronomy 4:24).

There are other references dealing with this same thought, but the point is, isn't it interesting that God revealed to Moses that not only is jealousy one of His divine attributes, it's also one of His names. What does it mean that God is a jealous God? Does He behave like the jealous husband who gets agitated if another man even looks at his wife? Is God like the jealous wife who becomes suspicious and bent out of shape if another woman smiles at her husband? Not at all. God is not fleshy and carnal like a lot of people we know. But God is jealous.

The word *jealous* would be better understood as meaning *zealous or impassioned*. It has the meaning of extreme devotion and denotes an intense loyalty. It also means passionately faithful. I don't know about you, but I'm glad to know God is zealous, impassioned, extremely devoted, intensely loyal and passionately faithful toward us. Hallelujah!

I'm thrilled to know that God feels this way about me, that His faithfulness, His love and devotion concerning me are extreme and intense. I certainly wouldn't be pleased if He were wishy-washy, lukewarm, half-hearted or occasionally interested in me. It gives me great peace of mind to realize that God is absolutely devoted to me and has given 100 percent of Himself to me. Indeed, to prove His loyalty and His faithfulness to me, He has drawn up a legal, binding contract, a covenant spelling out in exact terms—with no loopholes—how He will relate to me. This covenant outlines what He's willing to do for me, to be for me and what He desires to make available for me. The Bible reveals that God has bound Himself by an oath and a promise to convince us that He keeps His promises.

GOD IS ZEALOUS, IMPASSIONED, EXTREMELY DEVOTED, INTENSELY LOYAL AND PASSIONATELY FAITHFUL TOWARD US.

God also bound Himself with an oath, so
that those who received the promise could
be perfectly sure that He would never
change His mind. So God has given both His
promise and His oath. These two things are
unchangeable because it is impossible for
God to lie... (Hebrews 6:17-18 NLT).

Knowing these immutable facts about God, the question then is not: Is God fully committed and passionately devoted to me? The question is: How committed am I to the Lord and to His ways?

How surrendered am I to Him? What is the level of my faithfulness, my devotion to Him? Am I aglow and burning with zeal toward God and His things? The sad truth is that many believers in the American church are simply going through the motions when it comes to their involvement with their local church and in their personal relationship with God. Their Christian life has become a dreary exercise in futility. Where is our passion for God? What has become of the joy of our salvation that we basked in when we first came to Jesus and realized that He loved us and sought us out to make us His own?

So many believers today are guilty of the same faults that Jesus spoke of in the church in Ephesus when He visited John on the Isle of Patmos and gave him what we know to be the Book of Revelation. Jesus had some good things to say about this church, but He also let them know He had some things against them. Like so many today, they left their first love (Revelation 2:4-5). These Ephesian believers were doing good works. They took a strong stand against evil. They exposed false prophets, and they endured with patience and didn't turn their backs on Jesus when the going was tough. All these things were certainly admirable qualities in a Christian's life. But after commending them for their good works, Jesus said, "Nevertheless, I have somewhat against thee, because thou has left thy first love. Remember therefore from whence thou art fallen, and repent, and do the first works" (Revelation 2:4-5).

This church had committed a major sin, but it was not some evil works of the flesh. Rather, the church at Ephesus was guilty of sins of the heart. Through the years the believers had become caught up in the work of the ministry, but somehow they drifted away from loving Jesus Himself. They had become so devoted to service, they neglected the One they were serving—the very one in whose name all these good works were performed. *First love* means to love first. That means to love more than anything else, that everything else in our lives occupies second place. A Christian who is fully surrendered to Jesus is one who loves Him first and foremost above anything or anyone else in his or her life. The King of Glory must hold a place that nothing or no one else can touch or even come close to in terms of our love and our devotion.

Earlier I discussed the Bible truth that God has gone to great lengths to demonstrate His faithfulness to us. Hebrews 6:18 says that it was by two immutable, or unchangeable things, namely, God's oath and His promise that it is impossible for Him to lie. Because He has done this, we can be greatly encouraged and take comfort in the fact that God is a covenant-keeping God; He is the faithful God.

This biblical concept of covenant serves as one of the greatest illustrations of the power of surrender. A blood covenant was, and is, the most solemn, most sacred arrangement upon which two individuals could ever embark. A covenant in blood is a binding agreement that spells out in precise terms how two parties will relate to each other for the rest of their lives.

In ancient times, individuals would agree to enter into covenant with each other for a number of reasons: to underscore the importance of their mutual love and friendship, to ensure protection of a weaker tribe against a more powerful one, or simply to unite in a common cause or a mutual interest. In the Bible we see the example of Jonathan and David entering into covenant together as an expression of the brotherly love they felt for one another.

Once it was agreed that the two parties were willing to unite in a covenant relationship, the partners would undergo an elaborate ceremony filled with rich, spiritual symbolism. There were variations on each aspect of the ceremony, but generally each party would exchange articles of clothing, such as a belt or other item. Sometimes weapons were exchanged. Covenant oaths consisted of very solemn and irrevocable promises outlining in specific detail what each partner was willing to do or to provide for the covenant friend. Given the seriousness of a covenant agreement, one would never enter into this relationship lightly, or without serious thought and consideration. This compact was so binding and sacred, that if the terms of the covenant were not kept, the one failing to keep the oath could be required to forfeit his or her life.

The climax of the covenant ceremony consisted of the partners each making an incision, usually upon the palms of their hands until blood flowed. The bleeding palm of each member's hand would then be pressed together, skin against skin, blood against blood, resulting in the inter-mingling of each other's life-sustaining blood. The bloody flesh of the palms pressed together, and the blood of one partner entering the bloodstream of the other partner was very significant because blood represents life. Without blood, there can be no life.

Leviticus 17:11 reads, "For the life of the flesh is in the blood." Knowing this, it is obvious that this holy exchange of blood between two willing partners was their way of saying, "I pledge my life and all it represents to you. All that I have, all that I am, and all I am able to do, I hereby make available to you." The exchange of blood symbolized two lives merging into one. Although each member continued to retain his individual identity, by means of the blood covenant relationship the two were now joined together in spiritual union.

This covenant custom of pressing the palms of the hands together is with us even today. The popular Western habit of two persons greeting one another with a handshake grew out of this part of the ceremony. In our modern culture, we don't even give a friendly handshake a second thought. We instinctively reach out our hand to another simply as a way of offering our friendship and saying hello. And yet, symbolically it represents an all-important covenant exchange of blood in earlier cultures.

Can you understand now the concept of surrender that is so implicit in the covenant ceremony? Every aspect of this holy ritual speaks of total surrender. The oaths, the exchanges and the act of sharing one another's blood all taken together symbolize the ultimate act of submission and surrender to another. If you and I have entered into this biblical rite together with God, through the blood of Jesus, then we have professed that our lives are no longer our own. Our possessions are as much God's as they are ours. Our abilities and talents are now at His disposal. We are His, and He is ours.

Our relationship with God is not based on what our particular denomination believes about God. It is not based on our feelings. Our relationship with God is based on the blood of an everlasting covenant that Jesus shed on Calvary for us. The blood that flowed from Jesus' wounds as He hung suspended between heaven and earth was righteous blood. It was the blood of God; it was covenant blood.

The act of Christ freely yielding His life to establish a New Covenant between God and man was the ultimate example of surrender. God literally gave all He had in order to bring us back to Him. And now in return, all He asks of us is that we be willing to surrender our hearts to Him. He asks this not even for selfish reasons, but so that He can breathe His very own life and power in us. God wants to give us the greatest life we could ever imagine, a life that becomes available when we are willing to turn over the reigns of our life and put them into His all powerful hands.

The problem is, however, that the whole concept of surrender to Christ is so foreign in our modern, Western approach to Christianity. We are too caught up in materialism, recreation and selfish pursuits to be bothered by old-fashioned ideals such as sacrifice, denial and surrender. We seem to have the idea that these godly principles were meant for *other* people. Perhaps they were for those who lived in Bible times or for less civilized people in faraway lands, but certainly they are not for us as sophisticated Western Christians. But friend, if this is our thinking we are dead wrong.

Unconditional surrender to Jesus Christ is really entry-level Christianity. At least that's what Jesus had in mind when He shared the following words with Peter and the other 11 disciples.

> If any man will come after me, let him deny himself, and take up his cross, and follow me. For whosoever will save his life shall lose it: and whosoever will lose his life for my sake shall find it (Matthew 16:24-25).

That seems clear enough, wouldn't you agree? Jesus made this concept simple enough for anyone to grasp. If you want to follow Jesus and be His disciple, you must be willing to turn from your ways and your ideas about things and take up your cross and follow Him. That means there will be certain things you must say no to in your personal life. You must have a willingness to deny your flesh certain cravings and desires that could weaken your relationship with the Lord. Quite obviously, there are urges, and lusts of the flesh that, if acted upon, could take you to places you have no business being. You must realize that the enemy uses these kinds of things to lure you into deception and sin.

The idea of denying yourself doesn't just have to do with things that are sinful or just plain wrong. It also includes situations where decisions must be made and courses of action taken. Perhaps you're wondering: *Which way should I go? What path should I take?* So often we make decisions based solely on how it will affect us. Yet, it's important that you understand that some choices affect others besides you. Are you and I willing to take into consideration the question, *How will my decisions affect the people around me?* Remember, God not only wants the best for you, He wants to use your life to bless the maximum numbers of people in your sphere of influence.

Notice also that the second requirement Jesus sets forth for a true disciple is found in Luke's Gospel, where Jesus is quoted as saying "take up your cross daily." Daily means every day of your life, but what does it mean *to take up our cross* on a daily basis? The cross was an instrument of death, and criminals were executed on wooden Roman crosses. People died on them, and death by crucifixion was not a pleasant experience for the unfortunate victim. Everything inside the condemned criminal awaiting this torture recoiled at the prospect of this agonizing and excruciating means of capital punishment.

So, then, why would Jesus instruct us to carry a cross as a prerequisite for true discipleship? He does so because walking with Jesus and fully surrendering our lives to Him means that there will be things in our life that must die a painful death. In other words, we must be willing to relinquish our thoughts, plans and purposes in exchange for His.

We're so accustomed to relying solely on our own thoughts and trusting in our own ways as we walk through life. We're so used to steering the ship of our life, but the Bible declares that God's thoughts are higher than our thoughts; His ways are higher than our ways. They are higher and better than our own thoughts and ways (Isaiah 55:8-9), and they *always* bring about a greater blessing for us and those around us than we could ever imagine.

Knowing these things, we dare not allow the fatal sin of pride to prevent us from living in God's ways and thoughts. In fact, one definition of the word *righteousness* as it applies to the things of God could be defined as "His ways of being and doing right." Actually, I've learned something very important about the nature of God in the years I've walked with Him. It seems so obvious that you would think everyone already knows it. It's this: God is right about everything!

There's no subject in heaven or on earth that God does not know absolutely everything about; He's way smarter than the most intelligent human being on the planet many times over. If it were possible to assemble the brightest minds of those now living and all who have passed on, those we classify as geniuses, still their collective wisdom and knowledge would pale in comparison to what God knows.

> Wherefore God has also highly exalted him [Jesus], and given him a name which is above every name: That at the name of Jesus every knee should bow, of things in heaven, and things in earth, and things under the earth; And that every tongue should confess that Jesus Christ is Lord, to the glory of God the Father (Philippians 2:9-11).

There is coming a day when every human being who has ever lived, saint and sinner alike, will acknowledge that Jesus Christ is Lord of all. Wouldn't it be much wiser to acknowledge that fact now rather than when it becomes too late to do so? The act of unconditional surrender to the lordship of Jesus is simply our willingness to turn over control of our lives to the One who formed us in our mother's womb. Surrender to God enables us to resist the oldest temptation in the world and the deadliest temptation since time began. Men and women have wrestled with this temptation since Adam and Eve in the Garden of Eden. It is the temptation to act independently of God—the temptation to believe you know more than God.

> **THE ACT OF UNCONDITIONAL SURRENDER TO THE LORDSHIP OF JESUS IS SIMPLY OUR WILLINGNESS TO TURN OVER CONTROL OF OUR LIVES TO THE ONE WHO FORMED US IN OUR MOTHER'S WOMB.**

The act of surrender to God is a journey, not a one-time decision. There always will be selfishness to overcome. Surrender does not begin with our giving up something outwardly first, but it begins in the heart. It begins with the yielding of our hearts to God's will for our lives and bowing the knees of our innermost being to Christ. The more we try to hold on to and control things, the more we become slaves to the flesh nature and to our un-renewed minds, and the more miserable we become.

We find ourselves in the unhappy position of being a prisoner to that driving urge of having to control every aspect of our lives. This desire for self-control instead of yielding to the gentle leadership of the Good Shepherd is the underlying cause of so much stress in our lives.

Many are unwilling to surrender because they misunderstand the whole process. What does it mean to fully surrender to God? Let me tell you what it is not. It is not a passive resignation, an attitude of fatalism or an excuse to be spiritually lazy and just leave everything up to God. Nor does it mean that we stop thinking and simply go about our business as robots under God's command. The Lord gave us our minds, and He intends that we use them. Romans 12:2 informs us that we become transformed by the *renewing* of our minds, not by the *removal* of them.

In the kingdom of God, surrender to a loving and all-wise heavenly Father is always a voluntary act that results in your betterment. True submission can never be forced because it is something of the heart. It is an inner attitude of trust and obedience. It can never be demanded; it must be freely given. We must choose to surrender to Him. And when we do, we can become confident that we won't lose our uniqueness. We won't be required to abandon our personality and become someone else. Our personalities are unique, and God can use them in a sanctified way to give expression to the one-of-a-kind creation He made us to be.

Rather than your personality becoming diminished, the act of surrender to the Lord actually enhances your personality. You become free to be the person God intended you to be in the first place. Only God knows what your true destiny was meant to be in Him. Yielding to God brings freedom, not slavery. Why? Because the truth is, God is absolute life, absolute light and absolute love. In Him is no darkness at all (1 John 1:5); His ways are tried, tested and proven.

The only way He can bring about His deepest work in you is through the avenue of personal surrender to Him. The more we try to control our own destiny, the more frustrated we become. The more we try to hold on to our own ways and carry out our own plans, the more we find ourselves mired in disappointment and failure. We end up feeling buried beneath burdens we were never designed to bear. But the good news is, Jesus wants to lift those burdens and weights from our shoulders and carry them for us. He wants us to live in His peace. The way of surrender is the way of true peace and joy.

The reality is that all of us sooner or later will surrender to something. If we fail to yield to God and to His ways, we will eventually surrender to other opinions, interests, philosophies and expectations. Or we will surrender to the love of money, to resentment, to fear or to our own pride and lusts that war against our souls. We were created to please God, to worship Him and to serve Him with joy and gladness. If we fail to fully offer our lives to Him, these other things will begin to usurp the place in our lives that only God can fill. Truly, surrender to God is not only the best way to live, it is the *only* way to live if we want to experience true freedom. The many alternatives that vie for our attention will surely lead us down a dead-end road of emptiness and disappointment.

The case could be made that the whole Bible is a message of surrender to God. It reveals the blessings and the triumphs of people who chose to fully yield to the Lord, and it discloses the unfortunate consequences that befell those who decided to take matters into their own hands and sing the song, "I Did it My Way."

How much wiser and better it is to learn from others' mistakes, to see where they went wrong and determine not to repeat the same missteps they made. The most miserable, frustrated people on earth are those who call themselves Christians, who go to church and listen to sermons about the blessings of obedience and surrender to the Lord, but then go out and make most of their decisions without even consulting the Lord. They chart the courses of their lives based on their own reasoning and feelings, others around them or what statistics dictate to them.

They rely on conventional wisdom or on common sense, all the while failing to realize that God already knows what we're supposed to be doing. He doesn't rely on common sense. He has "uncommon sense" because He already knows the end from the beginning. He is the God who dwells in eternity (Isaiah 57:15), which means He operates outside the confines of space, time and matter.

He has perfect knowledge of past, present and future simultaneously at all times. When we come to that place of surrender to Him, we acknowledge the obvious: God is omniscient and we aren't. He is above all. He inhabits a high and lofty place, and we are finite and limited in understanding and knowledge. Our action of surrender to Him is our way of saying, "Lord, I give you permission to do in me, through me, for me and to me that which you have already ordained for my life. I give you the unqualified right to bring about the highest and the best in my life—that which you have had planned for my life before the world began."

God needs fully surrendered and obedient vessels through whom He can carry out His plan for the redemption of mankind. His plan is so glorious and so wonderful, the full scope of it will be revealed only in eternity. His plan and purpose is one in which those who are fully surrendered to Him always will be in the right place at the right time doing the right thing. His plan will enable His followers to be used of Him to build up and expand His kingdom on the earth.

The real Church is one made up of believers who are willing to become fully surrendered to God in every area of their lives. Will the real, surrendered Church please stand up?

CHAPTER 11

VESSELS OF
RECOVERY

The second chapter of Acts records one of the greatest events in the history of God's dealings with mankind. In these chapters, God supernaturally brings His Church into being, accompanied by the sound of a rushing, mighty wind and cloven tongues of fire. That holy fire from heaven rested upon the 120 gathered in the Upper Room on the Day of Pentecost as the Church was clothed with the same ability of the Holy Ghost that Jesus Himself was clothed. God confirmed His Word as these brave men and women preached with miraculous signs and wonders. Truly, this was a Church that turned the world upside down.

Is it possible for us in our day to see the effectiveness, the boldness and the power of that first century church? When we read through the book of Acts and compare the early church with today's church, we become aware that something is missing. There is a quality absent in our churches today that was very much present in the first church—and it's something that must be restored. If we're ever going to witness once again the success of those first century believers, it's imperative that we recover and restore that which has been lost.

Jesus commanded them—and us—to go into all the world and preach the gospel to every creature. Yet, the only generation that fully reached its own for Christ was that first generation of believers. Even more amazing is the fact that they accomplished this feat without the advantage of radio, TV, Internet or jet travel. Consider their track record. Paul evangelized some 1,800 miles of territory throughout Asia Minor. Both Jews and gentiles alike heard the message of Christ as Paul carried out this daunting task in the space of two years. From the Middle East, he planted the seeds of the gospel along the major highways of what is now Europe and touched an entire generation for God.

Those early disciples of Jesus Christ took His words spoken to them literally. He told them, "You shall receive power after the Holy Ghost comes upon you" (Acts 1:8), and they believed it and received it. When the wind of the Spirit filled the room where they were sitting, those disciples realized Jesus had indeed sat down at the right hand of God. They knew He had fulfilled His promise to ask the Father to send the Holy Spirit to come on them in power, and they also knew this power had fully equipped them to evangelize the world.

Those 120 disciples walked out of the Upper Room with a touch from the hand of God. They had received a commission from the Master and they took it to the streets. Peter had the boldness to touch a man at the Beautiful Gate in Jerusalem who had been crippled for 40 years, saying, "such as I have I give unto you: in the name of Jesus Christ of Nazareth, rise up and walk." Peter believed he had received something real, something wonderful, and it produced results. More importantly, Peter was one among many disciples who took up the challenge to reach the uttermost parts of the world with the gospel.

Friend, our generation must recover this same zeal and power that marked the early church if we ever hope to duplicate the success in the closing hours of this age that they experienced in theirs. Here lies the pivotal question: Are you and I willing to be among those who help restore the power of God that has been noticeably absent in the church through past generations?

Jesus is not returning for a worn-out, broken-down religious machine. He's returning for a church that has the fire, the passion, the boldness and the purity that the first century church possessed. If you want to know the kind of church Jesus is coming back for, take another look at the church that He left.

Jesus said in Matthew 16:18, "Upon this rock I will build my church; and the gates of hell shall not prevail against it." If Jesus comes after anything less than what He started, then He would have failed. Reading through the book of Acts as the dead were raised, the blind received sight, the lame were made to walk and whole cities were stirred for God, what we see is an infusion of God's life being poured into human vessels. We don't see religion—we see *life*. Those rugged early believers did not merely repeat the faithless doctrines learned in a seminary. They ministered in the power of the Holy Spirit.

God is dealing with the Church in this hour to recover truths that have been lost—truths that produced mighty results then and truths that will impact our world in a mighty way today.

1. THE FIRST GENERATION BELIEVERS WERE AWARE THAT TO BE FILLED WITH THE HOLY SPIRIT WAS NOT A ONE-TIME EXPERIENCE, BUT RATHER A CONTINUAL DRINKING IN OF LIVING WATER.

Paul exhorted believers in Ephesus to be filled with the Spirit (Ephesians 5:18). Notice that he did not instruct them to "get filled." He exhorted them to "be filled." The people who made up the core of this great Ephesian church first received the Holy Spirit in Acts 19, when Paul made his first missionary journey to that part of the world. It would be reasonable, therefore, to assume that many, if not most, of the believers in that church already had experienced the initial infilling of the Holy Spirit. So in Ephesians 5:18, Paul was not encouraging them to receive the baptism of the Spirit, rather he was exhorting them to maintain an ongoing fullness of God's Spirit in their lives.

Centuries before theologians began to construct a belief system of the Christian faith based on their own biased interpretation of the scriptures—long before there were Baptists, Methodists, Lutherans, Catholics, Presbyterians, Charismatics or any other sectarian Christian group—there existed a church that strongly believed in cultivating a dynamic relationship with the Holy Spirit. That church believed and practiced the blessing of staying full of His power at all times.

The Bible records four instances after the initial outpouring of the Holy Spirit in Acts 2 when believers experienced a re-filling of the Spirit: Acts 4:8, 4:31, 13:9 and 13:52. These were definite and powerful experiences of a perpetual infilling of the Spirit's power in their lives.

To better understand Paul's exhortation to be "filled with the Spirit" in Ephesians 5:18, consider the verse as translated in The Amplified Bible. It reveals a clearer understanding of what Paul was endeavoring to convey, when it says, "... ever be filled and stimulated with the Holy Spirit." This verse is again made clear when we look at the Greek language from which it was translated into the King James Version. I quote Kenneth S. Wuest, the late teacher emeritus of New Testament Greek at the famed Moody Bible Institute:

> *Filled* is *pleroo* [Greek], which means to fill up, to cause to abound, to furnish or supply liberally, to flood, to diffuse throughout. In Acts 6:15 we have Stephen, a man filled with faith and the Holy Spirit. Faith filled Stephen in the sense that it controlled Him. The Holy Spirit filled Stephen in the sense that He controlled him. Therefore, the fullness of the Spirit has reference to His control over the believer yielded to Him. The verb is in the present imperative: "Be constantly, moment by moment, being controlled by the Spirit." [1]

How desperately the world needs a Church that is being constantly filled, energized and controlled by God's Spirit—not a selfish, fleshy company of whining, lukewarm Christians who attend church, but never allow the Word or the Holy Spirit to govern their lives.

In the Bible, oil is likened to the anointing of the Holy Spirit. When God instructed the prophet Samuel to anoint David to be King of Israel, he took with him to Bethlehem a horn of anointing oil. By the act of pouring the oil upon the young, would-be King of Israel, David, was from that moment set apart by the Lord to fill the office of king. When the prophet Samuel anointed David with the oil, the scripture says, "...and the Spirit of the Lord came upon David from that day forward" (1 Samuel 16:3).

> HOW DESPERATELY THE WORLD NEEDS A CHURCH THAT IS BEING CONSTANTLY FILLED, ENERGIZED AND CONTROLLED BY GOD'S SPIRIT—NOT A SELFISH, FLESHY COMPANY OF WHINING, LUKEWARM CHRISTIANS WHO ATTEND CHURCH, BUT NEVER ALLOW THE WORD OR THE HOLY SPIRIT TO GOVERN THEIR LIVES.

Later in Psalm 92, David wrote in verse 10, "I shall be anointed with fresh oil." In scripture we repeatedly see the connection between oil and the anointing of God's Spirit. In fact, oil lamps were used to furnish light before the advent of electricity. These lamps would burn brightly as long as one kept a good supply of oil inside the lamp. But when the level of oil was inadvertently permitted to run low, the wick of the lamp would begin to burn. If the wick continued to burn with no oil in the lamp's reservoir, soon the room would fill with smoke.

When the oil ran out, but the wick was still burning with a small residue of oil still on it, the wick was attempting to produce a flame all by itself. The wick was actually consuming itself. It was trying in vain to do something it was never designed to do. The wick was attempting to supply light and fire without the help of the oil. Think for a moment about how this analogy of the oil lamp illustrates the church's futile and frustrating efforts to obey the Great Commission apart from the help of the Holy Spirit.

If the supply of the Spirit begins to dwindle in the church, and we attempt to accomplish effective ministry by human effort apart from the power of the Holy Spirit, the result will be a lot of smoke and very little useful fire. More to the point, we are witnessing today in large part a lot of smoke and confusion and a pitiful lack of the fire of the Holy Spirit in current Church life.

Jesus did not pray to the Father to send forth the Holy Spirit to fill believers just so we could speak in tongues and experience some kind of an ecstatic feeling. We have been immersed in the Holy Spirit to make it possible for God to make His home in us and express Himself through us wherever we are. "As God hath said, I will dwell in them, and walk in them; And I will be their God, and they shall be my people" (2 Corinthians 6:16).

We were saved and filled with the Holy Spirit to provide a suitable habitation in which God could dwell in the earth. Our bodies are the temple of the Holy Spirit. We are not here simply to be doctors, lawyers, merchants or mechanics. This may be our vocation, but in reality we are here to present our bodies as a living sacrifice to the Lord and be vessels in which He can inhabit and express Himself to the world. This is who we are and why we are here; this is our purpose. When you don't know your purpose, you'll wander around in confusion, bewilderment and defeat.

The only way God can touch people around us is for Him to touch them through us. Jesus didn't send the Holy Spirit all over Galilee and Judea to minister to the people. He went to them. He touched them. He spoke to them. He took them in His arms. And Jesus still does that today through you and me. The first century Church understood that they needed to be ever filled with God's Holy Spirit if they were to successfully duplicate Jesus' ministry.

2. THEY KNEW THAT THE POWER THAT RESIDED IN THEM WAS FROM GOD.

...When Peter saw it, he answered to the people, Ye men of Israel, why marvel ye at this? or why look ye so earnestly on us, as though by our own power or holiness we had made this man to walk? The God of Abraham, and of Isaac, and of Jacob, the God of our fathers, hath glorified his Son Jesus; whom ye delivered up, and denied him in the presence of Pilate, when he was determined to let him go (Acts 3:12-13).

It's not enough to glibly quote scriptures to folks who need healing in their bodies. There must be power behind our words—there must be power in Christians who speak the Word. If we are to be successful in giving hurting people what they need, we must be confident that we do indeed have something to give them—something tangible. We must be in a position to give them a real, miracle power from heaven—not just words and certainly not sympathy. We must know we are vessels of God possessing power from Him. We must also never lose sight of the fact that this divine power is not given for self-promotion to elevate us into a celebrity status among people. Rather, it is the holy, pure power of God given to us to relieve suffering humanity.

Luke's Gospel records an incident in Jesus' ministry dealing with this idea of rightly understanding the purpose of supernatural empowerment, and the dangers that can befall one who fails to maintain a proper perspective of the reason God chooses us to be channels of His power. In Luke 10 Jesus appointed 70 disciples and sent them two by two into several towns with instructions to heal the sick and preach the kingdom of God. Upon completion of their mission, these 70 returned thrilled to learn that demons were forced to bow to the authority Christ had given to each of them.

Jesus responded to their exciting discovery by reiterating that He had indeed given the 70 disciples power and authority over all the power of the enemy. But Jesus quickly cautioned them to make sure their joy was based on the fact that their names were written in heaven, not in the power given them over demons. In fact, it's interesting to note that immediately after the disciples expressed glee over their domination of evil spirits through Jesus' name, the Lord quickly responded by telling them, "I beheld Satan as lightning fall from heaven." In other words, in a mild rebuke, Jesus was making the point to them, "I witnessed firsthand the same pride in Lucifer that's now trying to snare you." A careful study of Isaiah 14 and Ezekiel 28 pinpoints clearly that spiritual pride was the damning sin that ousted Lucifer eternally from the presence of God.

Even in our day, we have observed those with God's anointing on their lives fall from grace. In the recent past, we've seen men and women mightily used of God to proclaim the gospel; anointed preachers whose ministries touched thousands for Christ. God confirmed the Word they preached with miracles, signs and wonders. The overwhelming majority of the notable miracles of healing and deliverance during the great Healing Revival in the 1940s and into the mid-1950s were authentic, medically-verifiable miracles—not hype and exaggeration.

These gospel preachers started out well. Many answered the call of God with a deep humility and a readiness to obey God, and the Lord blessed their ministries as they proved themselves faithful and trustworthy in His sight. The crowds grew, the Lord continued to show Himself strong and the miracles became even more spectacular. There was no doubt that God was using these ministers in a mighty way. But some lost sight of the reality that they were merely a vessel that God was using to bring glory and honor to His name. Many who were once humble preachers became seduced by the sin of pride and deception, and the end result was that some lost their ministries and even died prematurely.

How could this happen? Undoubtedly, they yielded to the thoughts and suggestions of the enemy and opened the door for him to gain access into their minds. Satan's goal was not merely to beguile them and discredit their once fruitful ministries, but ultimately his plan was to destroy their lives and remove them from the scene altogether.

That is why Jesus cautioned the 70 returning disciples in Luke 10 to place a greater significance on the fact that their names were recorded in heaven than on the power they had been given to cast out devils. Jesus told them it would be better for them to esteem the much more glorious reality that they were recipients of God's unconditional love and grace. Jesus counseled them that if the vital link of sonship with God is ever broken through pride and arrogance, devils will not be subject to the disciples; the disciples will be subject to devils.

So how do we maintain union with God? We must stay full of the Holy Ghost and offer the sacrifice of praise to God continually (Hebrews 13:15). We must walk humbly before God and cultivate a separated, sanctified walk with Him. When we do, the devils always will be subject to us and not us being subject to them.

If we ever break our vital link with the Master—as many have—the unfortunate result will be a lot of fruitless religious activity. We'll have a form of godliness, but no real power from heaven. People will come to our churches sick, lost and confused, and they will leave the same way they came.

The believers in Acts knew the power that flowed from them was not their own. Peter was aware that he received something in that Upper Room from the hand of God; he knew it came upon him and changed him into another man. The Holy Spirit is as tangible and real as electricity, and thank God, He can transmit Himself through us. We can live Spirit-infused lives charged with supernatural power to change the world.

Another aspect of this great truth concerning the disciples' awareness that the power in them was of God—and not of themselves—was the fact they were fully conscious that this power or treasure must be housed in clean and holy earthen vessels.

Consider the vision recorded in Ezekiel 47. What the prophet Ezekiel saw in this supernatural visitation of God speaks precisely to the point we've been sharing thus far. Ezekiel saw a river flowing forth from the house of God. At first the waters were ankle deep, but as the waters continued on their course, they soon became knee high. Rising higher, the river reached a man's loins in depth, and ultimately, the river's depths were immeasurable. As the prophet pondered the meaning of this vision, he noticed that trees were growing on both sides of the river's banks. These trees had root systems that drank deeply from the river, a river that brought healing wherever it flowed.

To fully grasp the importance of this scripture, let me explain that many times in God's Word when trees are not described literally they are to be understood figuratively. For instance, in Ezekiel 47, the trees symbolize people who were deeply and vitally connected to and drawing life from the river flowing from God. Their roots received life and refreshing from the river that enabled them to flourish and grow strong. This mighty river of life that Ezekiel described is nothing less than an Old Testament foreshadowing or a type and a shadow of the Holy Spirit's role in the life of the New Testament believer.

Jesus echoed this theme of rivers of living water in John 7:37-39, where rivers of blessing, healing and power would flow forth from the hearts of believers. However, it's important to understand that if this mighty river of healing and deliverance is to flow unhampered and unhindered through the Church to touch a needy world, then the vessel from which it flows must be clean, pure and undefiled.

Even though supernatural rivers of the Holy Spirit's power flow from within us as believers, we must also realize that our bodies—the vessels or containers of these rivers—are not yet fully redeemed. Our bodies have not become glorified, and therefore, our flesh is still subject to corruption. Romans 8:23 tells us that we are still awaiting the full redemption of our bodies. That's why our hair turns gray, our eyes grow dim with age and our feet don't run as swiftly as they once did. The point is, no matter how much power exists within us, as long as we are on this earth we will always be contending with our physical bodies, with flesh that still wants to do wrong sometimes.

That's why so many Bible verses are devoted to the subject of sanctified living. The believers of the first church recognized that this treasure, this power given them by God, resided in earthen vessels that must be maintained in a sanctified manner. We must walk in the fruit of self-control and learn to keep our bodies under subjection. We simply cannot live any way we want, if we want to experience the power of God operating in our lives. This truth is especially important in the lives of ministers—those who have been called to preach and to display the Word of God through their lives and ministries.

One can master the *mechanics* of ministry, say all the right words of this Christian walk and even reach some measure of success, but sooner or later, if you're not living right, your sin will find you out. You cannot go to church on Sunday and act like Peter, James and John, then go home and act like the devil all week and not pay a price for living a phony double-standard. The Holy Spirit will not flow through a contaminated vessel. We must keep our bodies a fit dwelling place for the One Jesus called "the promise of the Father" (Acts 1:4).

> ...What agreement hath the temple of God
> with idols? for ye are the temple of the
> living God; as God hath said, I will dwell
> in them, and walk in them; and I will be
> their God, and they shall be my people.
> Wherefore come out from among them, and
> be ye separate, saith the Lord, and touch
> not the unclean thing; and I will receive you
> (2 Corinthians 6:16-17).

More than anything, God wants a Church set apart from the uncleanness of this present evil world; He wants people whose hearts are totally sold out to the will of God. God wants sons and daughters who love Him with all their hearts, souls, minds and strength, and who make it possible for God to show Himself mighty in all His glorious manifested presence. Friend, the tragedy is that if we do not have the tangible presence of God in our churches, then we'll have to settle for simply having services.

The early church didn't settle for services per se, so why should we? These believers had building-shaking, great-grace, fear-of-God-preaching, Pharisee-defying, souls-added-to-the-church-daily explosions of God's glory. What a contrast to our cut-and-dried, pre-formulated, planned-in-advance and carefully orchestrated program of announcements and song singing that we call worship, and finely crafted, three-point homiletically correct sermons that too often lack the Spirit's power and conviction.

> **IT IS THE GLORY OF GOD ... THAT WE MUST HAVE IN THIS HOUR TO COME DOWN AND FILL OUR SANCTUARIES WITH A PRESENCE SO IRRESISTIBLE THAT EVERY SINNER IN THE HOUSE RUNS TO THE ALTAR TO GET RIGHT WITH GOD. ...**

Do you long to leave behind merely attending church and instead experience holy *encounters* with the Lord? Are you hungry for the glory of the Lord that changes us from the inside out? Then what we desperately need, is an invasion of glory that fills us with a holy reverence of God and saturates our souls with His life and love. It is the glory of God—the holy fire of God—that we must have in this hour to come down and fill our sanctuaries with a presence so irresistible that every sinner in the house runs to the altar to get right with God and be transformed into a fearless soldier of Christ.

Sadly, rather than our sanctuaries being places where God's holy presence lingers like a sweet aroma and words of unction flow from righteous preachers to change people's lives forever, all too often what we hear and see are things that would make Paul and Peter rent their garments in righteous anger.

God help us to get back to Bible basics. The Word of God tells us that, "We have this treasure in earthen vessels, that the excellency of the power may be of God, and not of us" (2 Corinthians 4:7). Let's determine to be those who will possess our vessels, our bodies, with honor and continually be reminded that our bodies are temples—temples of the Living God.

Are there things in your life you've given place to, attitudes and behaviors that grieve Him and prevent Him from using you in a greater way? If so, it's time to make some adjustments, to examine yourself and do whatever it takes to once again be one He can show Himself through in the closing hours of the world as we know it.

3. THEY WERE PEOPLE OF INTENSE MORAL AND SPIRITUAL CONVICTION.

We are living in a day when there seems to be little conviction or moral clarity in our contemporary church life. A gradual, but noticeable decline of character and integrity in our present Western culture has crept into the Church in recent years. The glamorizing of selfishness, immorality and blatant immodesty so prevalent in today's media is now comfortably seated in our church pews.

When I was growing up in the mid 1950s in a small eastern Ohio town, the people in my neighborhood had stronger convictions about right and wrong than do many in our houses of worship today. A scripture in Revelation gives insight into the caliber of believers in the early church:

> ...They overcame him by the blood of the
> Lamb, and by the word of their testimony;
> and they loved not their lives unto the
> death (Revelation 12:11).

These were people who believed strongly and stood for truth and righteousness. And, if need be, they were willing to give their lives for the cause of Christ. No matter what it cost them, they went everywhere preaching the resurrection of Christ. For some it meant the sacrifice of their lives. The 12 Apostles of the Lamb, with the exception of John, died horrible deaths, and in doing so, they proved that their deeply held convictions were non-negotiable. They weren't interested in gaining fame, fortune or personal popularity in a culture marked by rampant heathenism and pagan practices. They weren't seeking to escape persecution for the Word's sake. They regarded physical suffering for the name of Jesus as a badge of honor.

But the church today allows circumstances and the desire for acceptance by the world to determine its level of conviction. We have witnessed the endorsing and advocating of certain moral issues the Bible calls abominations. History reveals that civilizations that embraced lawless and immoral social positions such as homosexuality, perversion, violence and cruelty eventually discovered that in doing so they sealed their own doom as a culture.

That first church did not deviate from the core beliefs of the Christian faith, but instead took a bold stand upon the Word of God. The prevailing creed they lived by was, "We ought to obey God, and not man." Indeed, the Bible is the very Word of God, and no preacher, pope or priest has the right to change God's Word in an attempt to explain its truths away or to justify his or her pitiful lack of godly zeal.

Daniel was forcibly exiled to Babylon, but the ways of Babylon never took hold of him. Joseph was taken against his will to Egypt as a slave, but he never internalized the worldly ways of Egypt. Both these men remained loyal to God, maintaining their intimacy and trust in the Lord even while living as forced subjects in a foreign land. As a result, both great heroes of faith experienced supernatural power from God, and both were promoted to high places of rulership and authority because they never let go of their allegiance to God. They never compromised their core, biblical beliefs even though they were surrounded by unbelievers and idol worshippers. What was *in* them was so much greater than the evil, ungodly forces that were around them.

The Lord will show mercy on one who isn't saved just to demonstrate His love, mercy and compassion. But, if you are a born again child of God, there must be a positive response from you of faith, trust and obedience to His Word.

4. THEY UNDERSTOOD THAT THE POWER THEY HAD WAS BASED ON THEIR POSITION WITH GOD.

> If ye abide in me, and my words abide in
> you, ye shall ask what ye will, and it shall be
> done unto you (John 15:7).

Power with God is based on our position with Him. There is really no such thing as neutrality with God. In other words, we deceive ourselves if we think we can maintain a casual, once-in-a-while relationship with God and still be right with Him. The reality is, we are either on fire for God and passionately pursuing His presence and fully consumed with Him and His things, or we're living a life of compromise and complacency. It becomes easy to allow activities, pursuits, and even companionship with others to draw us away from a full-fledged life of consecration and joy in the kingdom.

The third alternative isn't any better. When we've turned back from God, a condition we sometimes refer to as being backslidden, we literally slide backward in our closeness with Him. Technically speaking, the word *backslidden* is an Old Testament term, but it is commonly used to describe those who little by little, degree by degree begin to grow cool toward God.

Rather than stoking the coals and fanning the flame of God's presence in our lives by spending quality time with Him in prayer, feeding on His Word and waiting in His presence, too often we allow cares, troubles or even a preoccupation with worldly things to gradually cause us to draw back from the Lord.

Perhaps a person became offended or lost a precious loved one. Perhaps a relationship failed or a loved one suffered a serious illness or some other painful setback. Whatever it was, we can be sure the devil loves to exploit these kinds of unfortunate circumstances in our lives. He will do his best to persuade us that God was the cause of every awful experience we or our loved ones ever encountered when the truth is, God was working behind the scenes doing whatever He could to prevent every awful experience in the first place. We can also count on the fact that God was endeavoring to strengthen us, comfort us and preserve us while we were going through the negative attacks, so we would not be completely overwhelmed and defeated.

Friend, the devil is mean. He doesn't play fair. He is malicious, and he is treacherous. And many have succumbed to his wiles and have been so wounded in the process that they have turned their back on the God they used to love and worship. So be on guard all the more against Satan's relentless warfare against the saints—against you. The devil is determined to overthrow the faith of God's people by any means he can. He will use any device in his arsenal of evil weapons to undermine, and if possible, completely destroy our trust and confidence in God's goodness. The sad reality is that the enemy of our souls has a pretty good track record of success in achieving these aims.

Satan knows he cannot destroy God. He tried that once and was even successful in persuading a third of the heavenly host to join him in leading what turned out to be a failed angelic rebellion against God in heaven (Revelation 12:4,7-9). Knowing he is powerless to come against God, and fully conscious of the whipping Jesus put on him at the cross, Satan employs the only remaining strategy left to destroy the work of God. He comes against the saints of God and does everything he can with the help of his hordes of demons to demoralize us and wear us down with discouragement.

That is the reason why when you look at the Church today, as Jesus Himself did in Revelation 3 when He walked among the believers in the Church at Laodicea, He witnessed three levels of commitment to God. Jesus saw saints whose spiritual walks with God were hot, cold and, worst of all, lukewarm. Yet, consider this. Jesus' sternest rebuke and most severe warning was leveled at those believers who had lapsed into a lukewarm spiritual condition.

Nobody likes lukewarm. It's bland, unexciting and basically useless. Indeed, it's important to realize that lukewarm water started out as hot water. When it's hot, you can make a satisfying cup of tea or coffee with it. But when it's lukewarm, what good is it?

On the other hand, a cold glass of water can refresh us when we're hot and thirsty. Yet, what do most people do when they lift a glass of water to their mouth expecting a cool, refreshing drink only to discover the water is lukewarm? Most people would spit it out. And that is exactly the feeling Jesus had when He observed believers who had cooled off in their love for God, allowing themselves to be caught up in worldly materialism and pride.

The problem with the Church today is the fact that we are *in* this world, surrounded by its ungodly influences, constantly being seduced by its twisted and distorted value systems. The experience has been that the rotten world system has crept into the Church, but the reality is that we belong to God. We are governed by a higher law than the laws of this present, evil world. If I abide in Him and His Word abides in me, I can confidently expect to walk in the power and blessing of God.

> Wherefore come out from among them, and
> be ye separate, saith the Lord, and touch
> not the unclean thing; and I will receive you,
> And will be a Father unto you, and ye shall
> be my sons and daughters, saith the Lord
> Almighty. Having therefore these promises,
> dearly beloved, let us *cleanse ourselves*

from all filthiness of the flesh and spirit,
perfecting holiness in the fear of God (2
Corinthians 6:17-18; 7:1).

If you were to take all the promises in the Bible and compile
a book that contained only the promises of God, you would most
surely have yourself a best-seller. Yet, we must understand that
God's promises are conditional. They simply cannot be lifted out
of the context of their scriptural setting. Promises come to pass in
our lives when we fulfill the conditions that are attached to them.
Conditions to God's wonderful promises were inserted in scripture
for a very good reason. Conditions were not set forth in scripture
to make it more difficult to receive the promises, but conditions
were set forth in scripture to make it easier to receive. Friend, if
we fulfill the conditions, nothing can keep us from the promises.

The truth is, if we keep the conditions outlined in God's
Word, then nothing can keep the promise from coming to pass in
our lives. If we respond in obedience to God's Word, we position
ourselves to receive God's best. On the other hand, we could
quote the scriptures all day long, but until we obey the Bible
all our efforts will be in vain. Nothing will happen in our lives
until we act in faith and obedience to the promise of God we are
claiming.

So an important question becomes: How do we maintain our
all-important position with God? And to answer this question,
we must ask yet another one: How did Jesus do it? Outlined here
are examples of how Jesus walked in fellowship with heaven
while on the earth.

- **Priorities** – Jesus had His priorities straight. He
  cultivated and maintained an intimate fellowship
  and relationship with His heavenly Father *first* before
  anything else. Nothing in Jesus' life and ministry was
  permitted to supersede time spent with God the Father.

- **Prayer Life** – Jesus exhibited an amazing prayer

life, but not out of a sense of religious duty or legalistic obligation. His prayer life was based on an earnest desire to have fellowship with God and to connect with the mind, will and purpose God had for Him. The Gospels tell us that often Jesus would arise before dawn and go to a desert place, away from the crowds, away from His disciples and away from the demands of the day to make sure nothing interrupted time spent with His Father.

• **Deny the flesh, feed and empower the human spirit** – Jesus fasted on a regular basis to deny His flesh and enhance His spiritual walk. Perhaps we need to do the same because a Church ruled by the flesh will never do the works of Jesus.

Fasting is not to be regarded as some kind of bargaining chip with God, where we think, *I've gone without food for all these days God, so You owe me, God.* Fasting was never meant to be a sacrifice we impose upon ourselves in order to *make* God do something in our lives. As one minister rightly observed, God is the same before, during and after we fast. Fasting changes us because it is a means by which we keep our flesh under control.

5. THEY WERE TOTALLY IMPRESSED WITH JESUS.

It is possible to be excited about miracles and still be dead in sins. Many rejoiced and marveled when Jesus multiplied the loaves and fishes. They were amazed to see cripples walk and blind eyes receive sight. Yet, when Jesus began to deal with the crowds about the necessity of total commitment to Him, many turned and no longer followed Him.

We must recognize that an all-consuming passion for Jesus is what drove this first century church—not merely for what He did, but with whom He was. In many quarters today, Jesus has been relegated to second place. However, any church that elevates and promotes anything other than Jesus as the centerpiece of its existence is clearly missing the mark. If things like water baptism, the mass, prosperity or even speaking in tongues has assumed a greater prominence than a passionate love for Jesus, that church will veer off track. These are all important components of church life, but Jesus is to be the hub, the center of all we do and all we love.

The early church was totally impressed with Jesus. The believers lived for Him, and they were willing to die for Him. Their love for Jesus drove them to the uttermost, to imprisonment and for some even death. Early believers were so passionate and determined to carry the message of Jesus Christ that we often read of them beaten, persecuted, jailed and pressed beyond measure in their quest to preach Jesus.

Walking with Jesus and living a radical Christianity that arouses the world's attention will certainly not result in our experiencing a life of ease and comfort. Actually, it's quite the opposite. There will be times like Paul experienced when we'll be "troubled on every side" (2 Corinthians 4:8). However, like Paul we also can take great comfort in knowing that no matter what trouble we may face, God will deliver us just like He did this great apostle.

> **IF YOU ARE ANCHORED ON THE ROCK OF AGES, IF CHRIST IS THE FOCUS OF YOUR LIFE, YOU WILL BE ABLE TO STAND FIRM WHEN ALL THE OTHERS AROUND YOU ARE BEING TOSSED ABOUT AND SCATTERED.**

So many believers today are governed by circumstances, dominated by the seen and ruled by comfort and convenience. But if you are anchored on the Rock of Ages, if Christ is the focus of your life, you will be able to stand firm when all the others around you are being tossed about and scattered. Jesus was the first love of these early believers, and that love moved them beyond the ordinary into the extraordinary—from the natural to the supernatural.

Earlier, when we dealt with the words of Jesus to the Ephesian believers in the book of Revelation, we noted that

Jesus commended them for their many good works. But He also chastised them for allowing their love for Him to wax cold. Despite all the good things this church accomplished, the Lord made it clear they had allowed their good works to take on a higher value than their love for Jesus. The good news, friend, is that we don't have to choose between doing good works or loving Jesus. In reality, our intense love for the Master will compel us toward works of mercy and kindness.

Consider this example. When a man decides to marry and take a wife, he stops looking at all other women, or at least he should. He's done looking; he's found his woman. If the new marriage is to flourish, not merely *survive*, the groom must turn his complete attention to his bride. That's also the way the relationship between the Church and Christ was meant to be. That first church was in love with Jesus; He was their first love.

Statistics tell us that more than half of all Christian marriages today end in divorce and the top three reason are usually issues related to communication, sex and money. But in reality, I believe many couples have failed to keep their first love alive with each other. Unfortunately, as time goes by in a marriage, too many partners no longer pay as much attention to each other as they once did; they begin to take one another for granted. She's no longer that cute little cheerleader any more, and he's no longer that "hunk of burning love" he used to be. The downward spiral of taking one another for granted should serve as a serious warning sign in the marriage relationship. Likewise, when our passion for God begins to wane, we must be aware of the dangers of drifting away from the One who purchased us with His own blood.

If you were closer to Jesus in the past than you are right now, you should be very concerned. There's nothing more valuable than your relationship with Christ and your love for Him. If the fellowship you once shared with Jesus has dissipated, faded or blurred, you need to know it can be ignited once more. The more time and attention you give to something, the more your desire and passion for it will begin to increase. More specifically, the more of your attention, desire and time spent in God's presence, the more your love for God will grow and thrive.

6. THEY WERE WILLING TO MAKE ANY SACRIFICE NECESSARY TO FULFILL THE GREAT COMMISSION.

> For we cannot but speak the things which
> we have seen and heard (Acts 4:20).
>
> For though I preach the gospel, I have
> nothing to glory of: for necessity is laid
> upon me; yea, woe is unto me, if I preach
> not the gospel (1 Corinthians 9:16).

Those first believers were willing to make any sacrifice necessary to make disciples of all nations. They were willing to pay any price to make Jesus known; they counted the cost and rejoiced to be counted worthy to suffer for His name. In fact, their sacrifice and devotion illustrates for us an important element of effective world evangelism, which is this: *Nothing* can take the place of a personal witness for Jesus Christ. The majority of believers today can trace their new birth experience back to someone who took the time to personally share Christ with them, one-on-one.

Friend, our obligation to the great commission goes far beyond sending $10 to a ministry somewhere. You have a voice, and Jesus has strategically placed you where you are right now to touch this world with the goodness of God. The fact is, you're going to give your life for something anyway. What could be greater than devoting your life to the rescue of hurting people? Why not give your life for something that will far outlast your time on earth?

The lack of missionary zeal in our churches today is alarming. We must be willing to change the prevailing dynamics of contemporary evangelism. The programs and ministries that compose the bulk of contemporary church life are mostly designed to minister to the ones sitting in our pews. Yet, there's something wrong with that picture because our mandate is to *go*—not sit! Jesus said that the gospel must be preached to "all nations" and to "every creature." We have been destined to make God's love known to the whole world.

> Ask of me, and I shall give thee the heathen
> for thine inheritance, and the uttermost parts
> of the earth for thy possession (Psalm 2:8).

This first Church knew what asking the Lord for the heathen would involve. And, yet, what was true of Jesus when this Psalm was written is true of Him today. We are the body of Christ on the earth today; the vehicle through which He expresses Himself. To ask for the heathen meant that Jesus would suffer death at Calvary. For the apostles "to ask" would cost them their lives as well, but God gave them the heathen for their asking.

> That which has been is that which shall be
> again (Ecclesiastes 1:9).

God is raising up a vessel of recovery in these last days. God is a God of restoration. He has always reserved for Himself a remnant of people determined to follow Him regardless of what other people, even the majority of people, were doing. He has always reserved for Himself a people not influenced by the times, men and women full of godly conviction and fully surrendered to Him.

I believe God will startle this generation with the power of the gospel, but He must have a vessel in which He can flow through to accomplish His goal. If we provide Him a suitable vessel, the oil will never run out. But there must be a bold remnant who will stand up and cry, "The river is flowing in the wrong direction. We must turn it around." The real Church is one that is not afraid and not ashamed to admit it has lost its bearings. Let's be the generation that will change the course, turn the ship around and head it in the right direction.

(AUTHOR'S NOTE: I am deeply indebted to the late Rev. B.H. Clendennen for much of the source material used in this chapter. Brother Clendennen was an ordained minister of the Assemblies of God for more than 50 years. He was also an internationally known speaker, author and radio and TV minister. He founded the first School of Christ in Moscow, Russia, in 1992. The School of Christ has now reached into more than 100 nations. Brother Clendennen was promoted to heaven on December 13, 2009. He was a fearless and mighty soldier of the cross.)

CHAPTER 12

OUR
MOMENT
IN HISTORY

In much the same way that relay runners finish their portion of a race and pass off the baton to a teammate anxiously awaiting the opportunity to grasp it and run across the finish line, so the legacy of the gospel has been passed down to us. Each successive generation of believers since the first generation in Acts has had both the privilege and the responsibility of carrying the torch of Christ's ministry to the people of its generation. We are stewards of the mysteries of the kingdom of God in our day; the gospel has been placed in our trust.

> So then, let us [apostles] be looked upon as ministering servants of Christ and stewards (trustees) of the mysteries the secret purposes of God. Moreover, it is [essentially] required of stewards that a man should be found faithful [proving himself worthy of trust] (1 Corinthians 4:1-2 AMP).

A steward, or a trustee, is one who has been given the legal responsibility of overseeing the management of an inheritance, an estate or other things of value. A good steward wisely administers and cares for that which has been placed in his trust. Likewise, the Church has been entrusted with something far more valuable than silver and gold or property and lands. We have been given the responsibility of perpetuating Christ's ministry in our generation.

However, before we can effectively advance Christ's message, it's imperative that our concept of the Church match God's original concept for this mighty, living organism He raised up to bring deliverance to the world. The Church is nothing less than Christ in us, covered with flesh. Oh, that the Church would awaken out of its spiritual stupor and comfortable complacency and do and be what God destined it to be.

Yet, unfortunately, we've been raised in an atmosphere of such timid Christianity that many believers today breathe a sigh of relief if they make it through another week without anyone learning they are Christians. Too many Christians live like secret agents with a dual identity. They lift their hands and shout "amen" at church, but when they walk out the door, they do their best to blend in with the world. Their lives have become compartmentalized and arranged into a series of neatly organized boxes of existence. Instead of the Lord being the absolute center and focal point of all they do, sadly God is only real to them on Sundays.

Away with such meager concepts of who and what a Christian is. We've lived on such a low level of Christianity for so long, it has become accepted as normal Christian living. Genuine Christianity is radical. A Christian should not be a friend of the world and should not be interested in conforming to the world's twisted sense of right and wrong. *Don't allow yourself to be a faux Christian!* Refuse to buy into the imitation style of Christianity that has become the norm in so many circles. Don't accept any substitutes!

Let's be the generation that drives the nail into the coffin of a weak, worldly Christian faith. Let's not settle for a socially acceptable, politically correct, nonconfrontational religious social club. Let's arise as sons and daughters of God and go forth in our time to the lost and hurting people with fire from heaven and God's love burning in us.

God's truth is non-negotiable. Real faith does not—nor will it ever—adjust itself to fit the current standards of a sinful culture hostile to God and everything He represents.

> The human soul is ever lazy toward God,
> and no one generation has seemed to be
> able to travel very far on its way back to
> God and His standard from which the Early
> Church fell. It is true that human error or
> conceit continually satisfies itself with a part
> instead of the whole, but the real fact is
> that men are not willing to pay the full price
> to come back fully to God's standard, to be
> all the Lord's. The early Church came forth
> from the "upper room" fresh in her "first
> love," baptized with the Holy Spirit, filled
> with God, possessing both the graces and
> gifts of the Spirit, and with a one hundred
> per cent consecration for God.
>
> This was the secret of her power. She
> was all for God, and God was all for her.
> This principle will apply in all ages, both
> individually and collectively. No sacrifice
> on the altar means no fire. The fire of God
> never falls on an empty altar. The greater
> the sacrifice, the more the fire.
>
> When the prodigal gets home and the
> Church becomes one hundred per cent for
> God again, we will have the same power,
> the same life–and the same persecution
> from the world. The reason we have so little

persecution now is that the Spirit cannot press the claims of God home on the world through us. When that happens, men must either surrender or fight.

Jesus Christ, the same yesterday, today, and forever! God never changes. We have changed. We are not waiting for God. God is waiting for us.

The Holy Spirit is given; we are still in the dispensation opened on the day of Pentecost. But God can only work when we are willing, yielded, and obedient. We tie God's hands. ... When we are filled with our own ways, think ourselves rich and increased in goods spiritually, God can give us nothing.

The best preacher in the land cannot preach with liberty when his message is not desired or received. The oil ceases to flow as soon as there are no more empty vessels to be filled.[1]

Does it bother you at all to realize that the largest and most influential, evangelistic and mission-minded churches in the world are currently in Asia and Africa? What has happened to the Church in America? What has happened to God's blueprint of what the Church was intended to be as set forth in the book of Acts?

We should be provoked to righteous jealousy when we consider that churches in South and Central America, and Asia and Africa far outpace the church in America in following this New Testament example. At this point, it's entirely possible that there are more on-fire, sold-out-to-God, Spirit-baptized, Jesus-loving believers in China than in any other nation in the world. The spiritual children spawned there through Western missionaries preaching the gospel are making our American churches resemble spiritual morgues.

Our houses of worship in many places today resemble the prodigal son who took his father's rich inheritance and squandered it in a sinful, hostile world. At least he had enough sense—after losing everything and nearly starving to death—to return to his father's house with the hope that somehow he could be restored back to the good graces of a loving parent.

What will it take for us to realize how far we as a Church have strayed from our original purpose? Does God have to wait for another generation who will join forces with Him and cry out for the rain of the Holy Spirit that will usher in the awakening this nation desperately needs?

Friend, this is our moment in history—this is our time to shine!

> Arise, shine; for thy light is come, and the glory of the Lord is risen upon thee. For, behold, the darkness shall cover the earth, and gross darkness the people; but the Lord shall arise upon thee, and His glory shall be seen upon thee. And the nations shall come to thy light, and kings to the brightness of thy rising (Isaiah 60:1-2).

I'm convinced ours is the generation the prophet Isaiah was speaking of here. Has there ever been a time when darkness has shrouded our world more than we are seeing presently? Has there ever been a moment in history when such gross, unspeakable evil has gripped the people?

But, my friend, God knew these hard times were coming. Nothing ever has, or ever will, catch Him off guard. He is fully prepared to counter the unbelievable events taking place before our eyes, both here and abroad.

Here is the awesome truth that the Church needs to seize: God has prepared you and me to be the answer for these times. We carry His light in this dark world.

Look around you and understand that we are nearing the awesome climax of the war between the kingdom of God and the kingdom of Satan. It's time we're sold out to God 100 percent. There can be no fraternizing with the enemy. The Church has no other business than to communicate the gospel to the world in the power of the Holy Spirit.

Nothing but the zeal and the one hundred percent consecration of the early church, both in laboring for the salvation of the nations and in building up the one true world-wide Church, will or can satisfy God. He will accept no substitutes or compromise with our ideas and fleshly plans. There simply must be an utter abandonment to His full will and His great eternal purpose in His own children! ... I am convinced that God is going to put the church through the fire to destroy the dross. Judgment begins at the house of God. ... We are reaching the culmination of this age, and nothing but a practical application of the gospel can hope to survive. ... God can only defend obedience to His Word. Never fear—he *is* going to have a Church without spot or wrinkle. But do you and I want to have a part in it? A sectarian, competitive, selfish, self-seeking Church cannot survive. The Church *must* return to the spirit of the early church in the Book of Acts. She must yield to God and press into His present truth for this last hour. ... *Our God is a consuming fire!* [2]

Will the real Church please stand up?

APPENDIX

PREFACE

1. McDowell, Josh. *More Than a Carpenter.* Wheaton, IL: Living Books, Tyndale House Publishers, Inc., 1977; p. 26.

CHAPTER 1

1. The Schofield Reference Bible. New York: Oxford University Press, 1909, 1945, 1937, 1945; p. 1192.

2. Horton, Harold. *The Gifts of the Spirit.* Nottingham, England: Assemblies of God Publishing House, 1934; p. 14.

CHAPTER 3

1. Bartleman, Frank. *Another Wave of Revival.* Springdale, PA: Whitaker House, 1982; p. 140.

2. Chadwick, Samuel. *The Way to Pentecost.* London: Hodder and Stoughton Limited, 1932.

3. American Dictionary of the English Language. San Francisco, CA: G. & C. Merriam Company, 1967, 1995; p. 41.

4. *Full Life Bible Commentary to the New Testament.* Grand Rapids, MI: The Zondervan Corporation, 1999 pp. 635-636.

5. Vincent, Marvin. *Word Studies in the New Testament*, Vol. 1. Peabody, MA: Hendrickson Publishers, 1886; p. 551.

6. Lindblade, Frank. *The Spirit Which Is From God.* Second

Printing. Pensacola, FL: Christian Life Books, 2008; p. 12.

7. *Vessels of Recovery*, Audio sermon by Rev. B.H. Clendennen.

CHAPTER 4

1. The Holy Bible, Authorized King James Version. Nashville, TN: Broadman and Holman Publishers, 1987; p. 998.

2. Bosworth, F.F. *Christ the Healer.* Old Tappan, NJ: Fleming H. Revell Company Publishers, 1973; pp. 53-54.

CHAPTER 5

1. Horton, Harold. *The Gifts of the Spirit.* Nottingham, England: The Assemblies of God Publishing House, 1934; p. 7.

CHAPTER 8

1. Blaise Pascal, Pensées, Page 181, Published Posthumously in 1670.

CHAPTER 11

1. Wuest, Kenneth S. *Word Studies in the Greek New Testament.* Grand Rapids, MI: Wm. B. Eerdmans Publishing Company, 1973; pp. 127-128.

CHAPTER 12

1. Bartleman, Frank. *Another Wave of Revival.* Springdale, PA: Whitaker House, 1982; pp. 136-138.

2. Ibid, pp. 151-152.

HOW YOU CAN BECOME PART OF THE REAL CHURCH

Through the pages of this book, you've read about the real church. The real church is composed of people just like you who have made the most important decision one can ever make—the decision to make Jesus Christ the Lord of their lives.

Are you ready to encounter the power and presence of the Living God? Are you prepared to face eternity? You can be. It's simple, and its only one prayer away. You can choose to receive Jesus as Lord and Savior right now by praying this simple prayer out loud. Your life will never the be the same again.

Dear heavenly Father:

Your Word says, "Whosoever shall call on the name of the Lord shall be saved" (Acts 2:21). I call on You right now. The Bible also says if I confess with my mouth that Jesus is Lord and believe in my heart that You have raised Him from the dead, I shall be saved (Romans 10:9-10).

I make that choice now!

Jesus, I believe in You. I believe in my heart and confess with my mouth that You were raised from the dead, and I ask You to be my Lord and Savior. Thank You for forgiving me of all my sins. I believe I'm now a new creation in You. Old things have passed away; all things have become new in Jesus' name (2 Corinthians 5:17). Amen.

If you prayed this prayer today, please share the good news with us!

Montgomery Ministries
P.O. Box 2707
Broken Arrow, OK 74013
918-760-1380
monty1949jim@gmail.com
www.montgomeryministries.net